It happens that nothing is obvious anymore.

ornela vorpsi

NOTHING OBVIOUS

Scalo Zurich – Berlin – New York

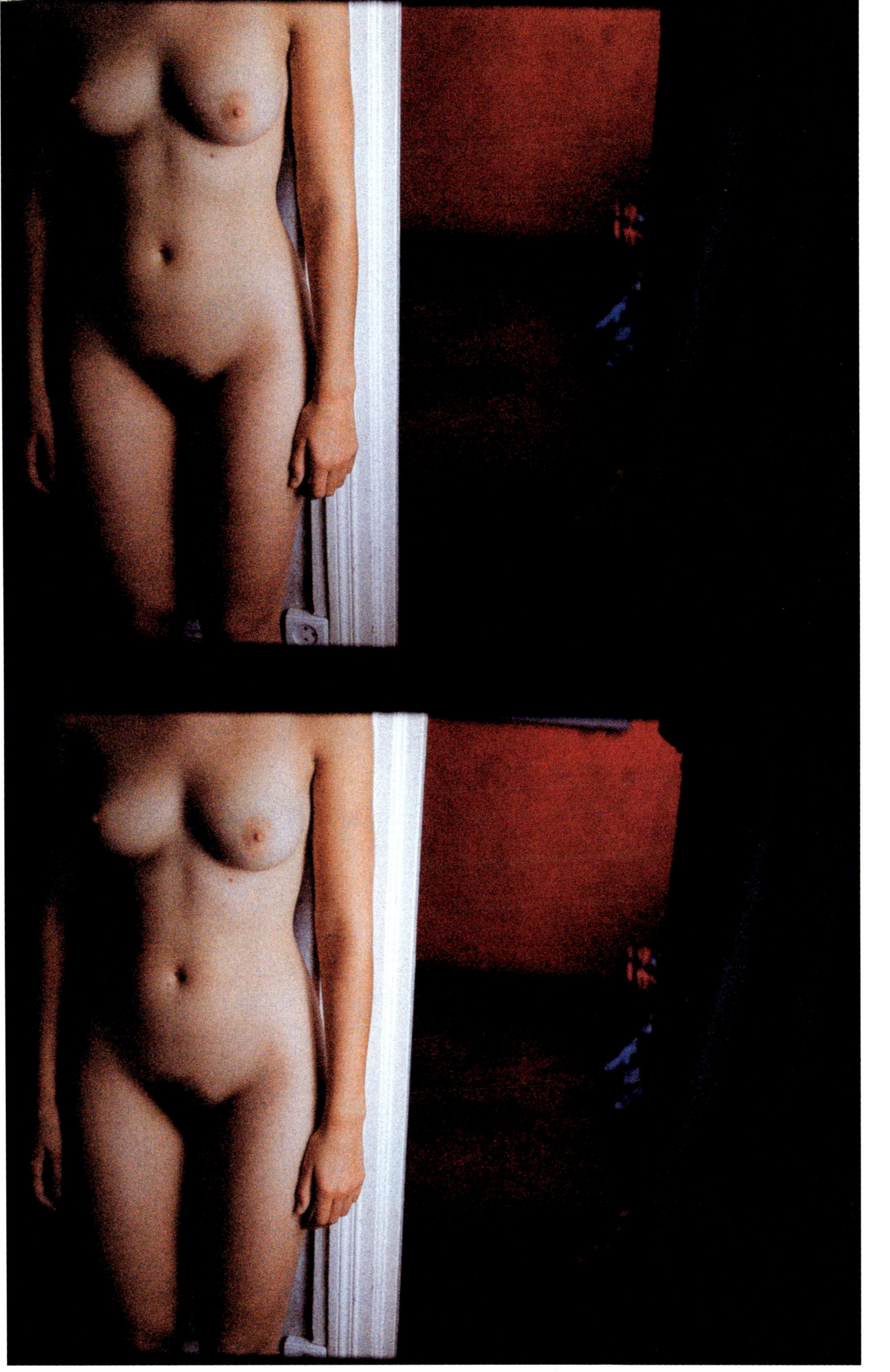

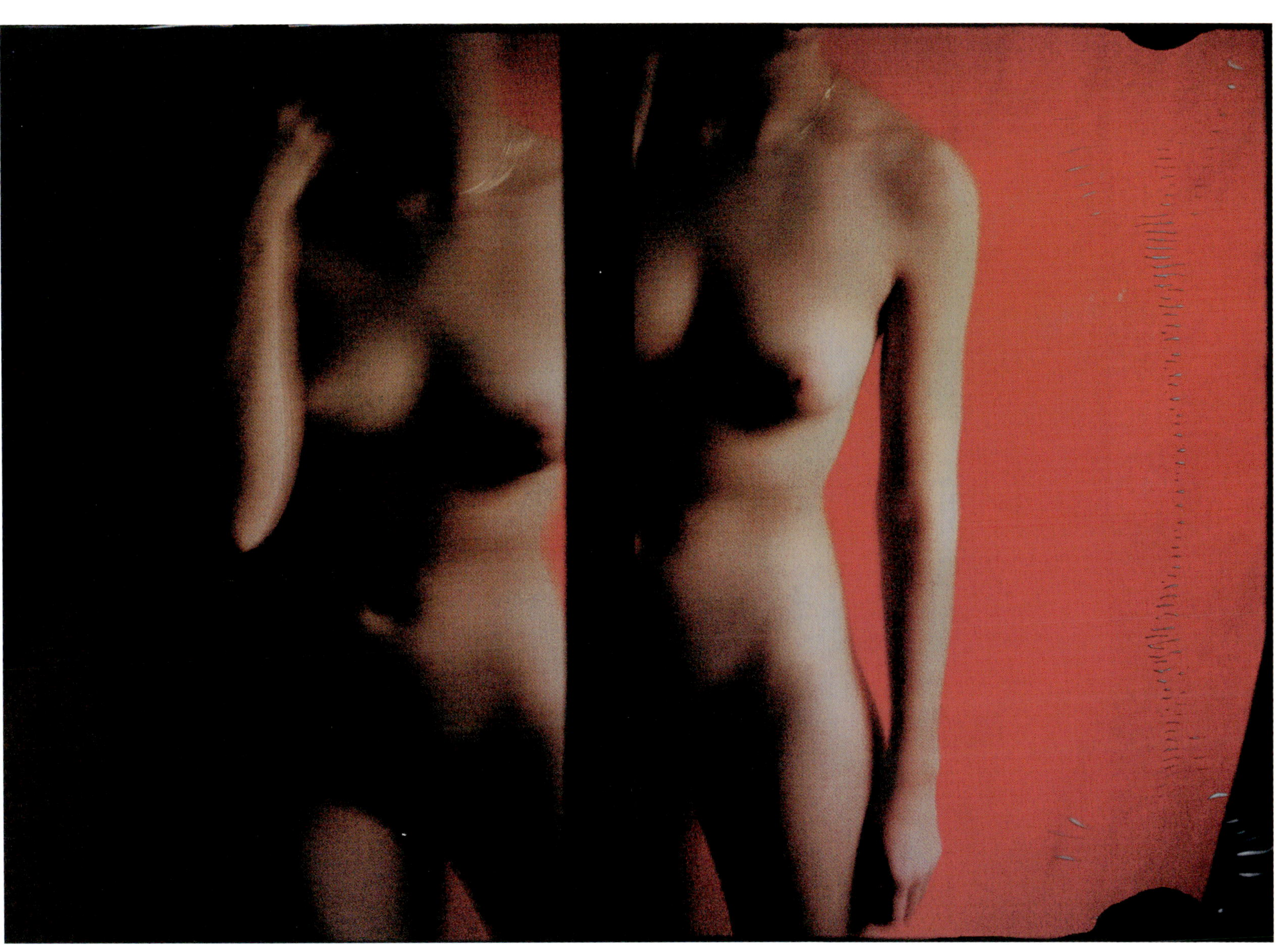

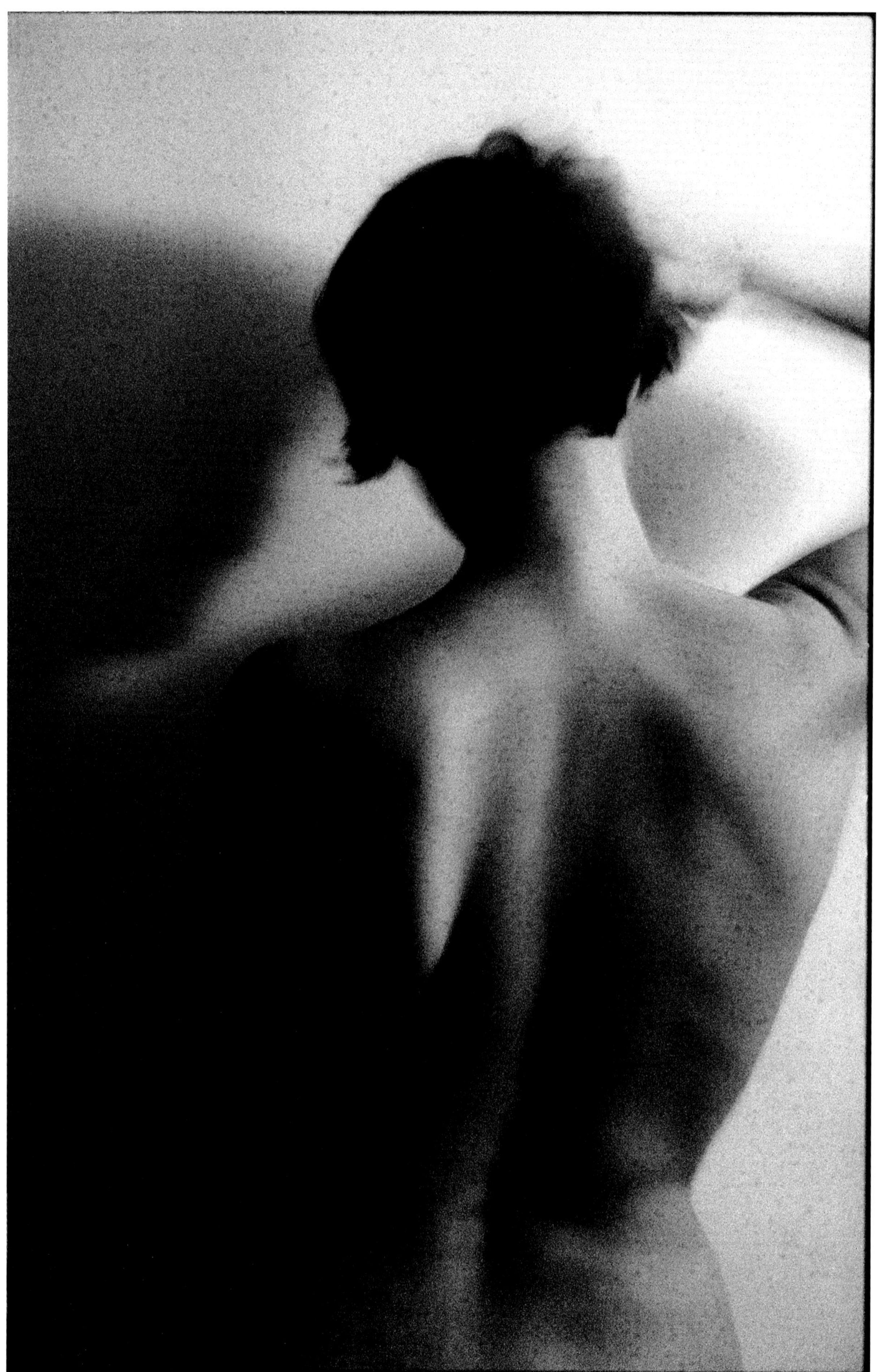

A little brown window refracting the sky. Rain. Today, my body belongs to me. The warmth of the watered dust has the power to calm. I accept my veins and my heart and their caprices. For a fraction of a second, I am convinced that I cannot live without this vice, this useless thing that is pure egoism. (Art.) It is like obsessively coddling yourself, like being able to understand that you exist, like knowing you can move endlessly through open spaces and closures in a kind of madness that liberates you from the tiresome slavery of thinking.

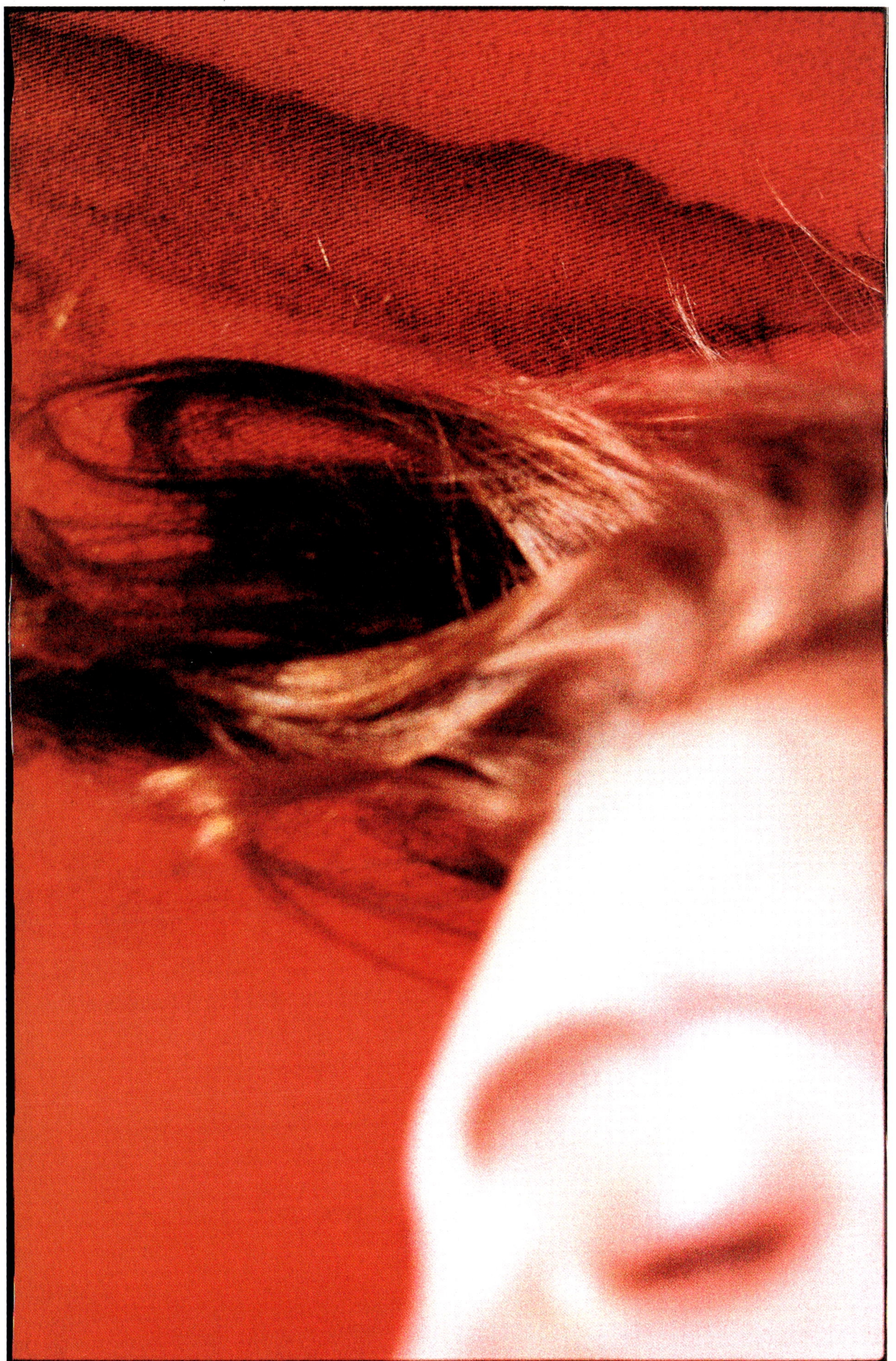

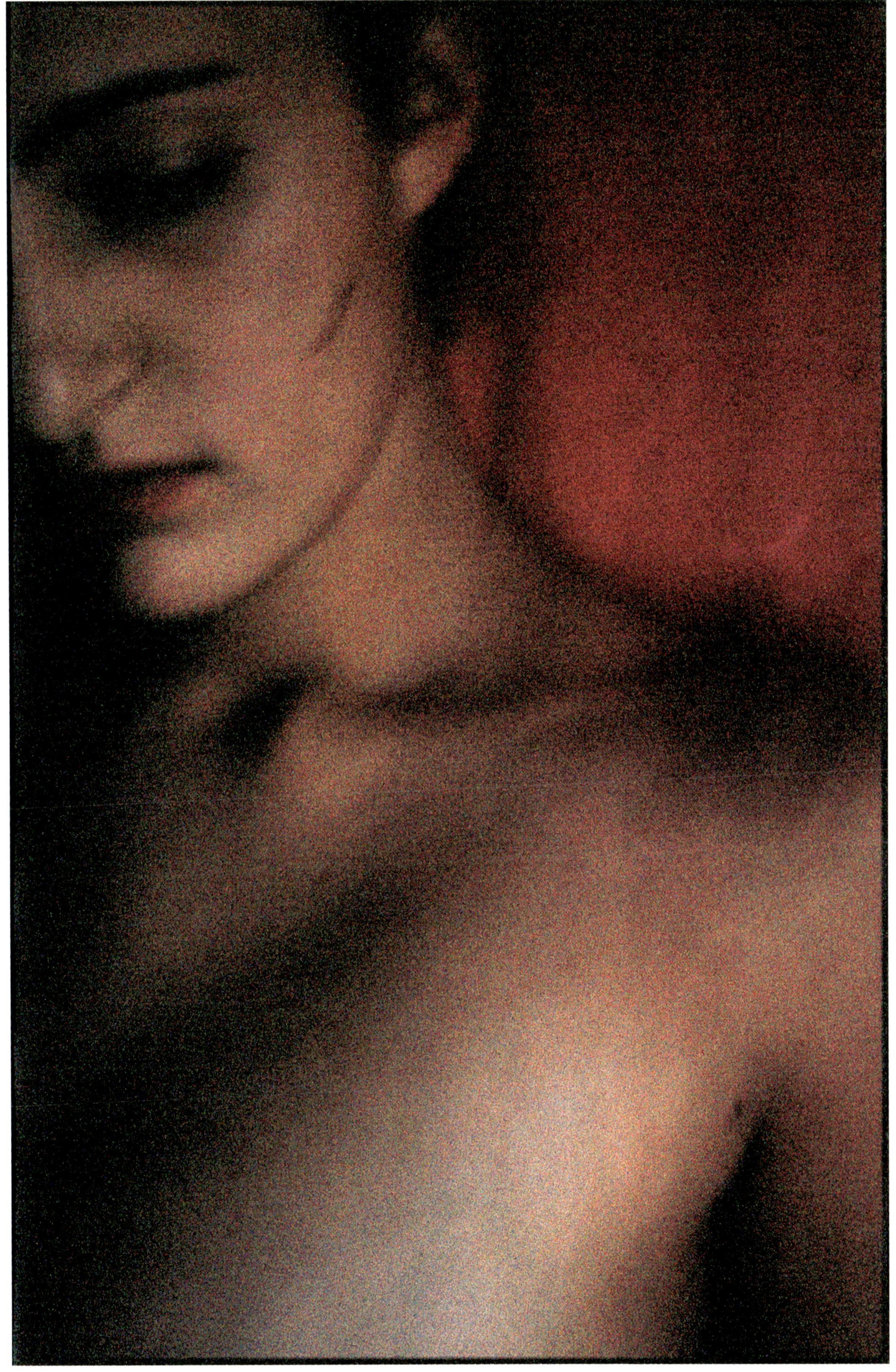

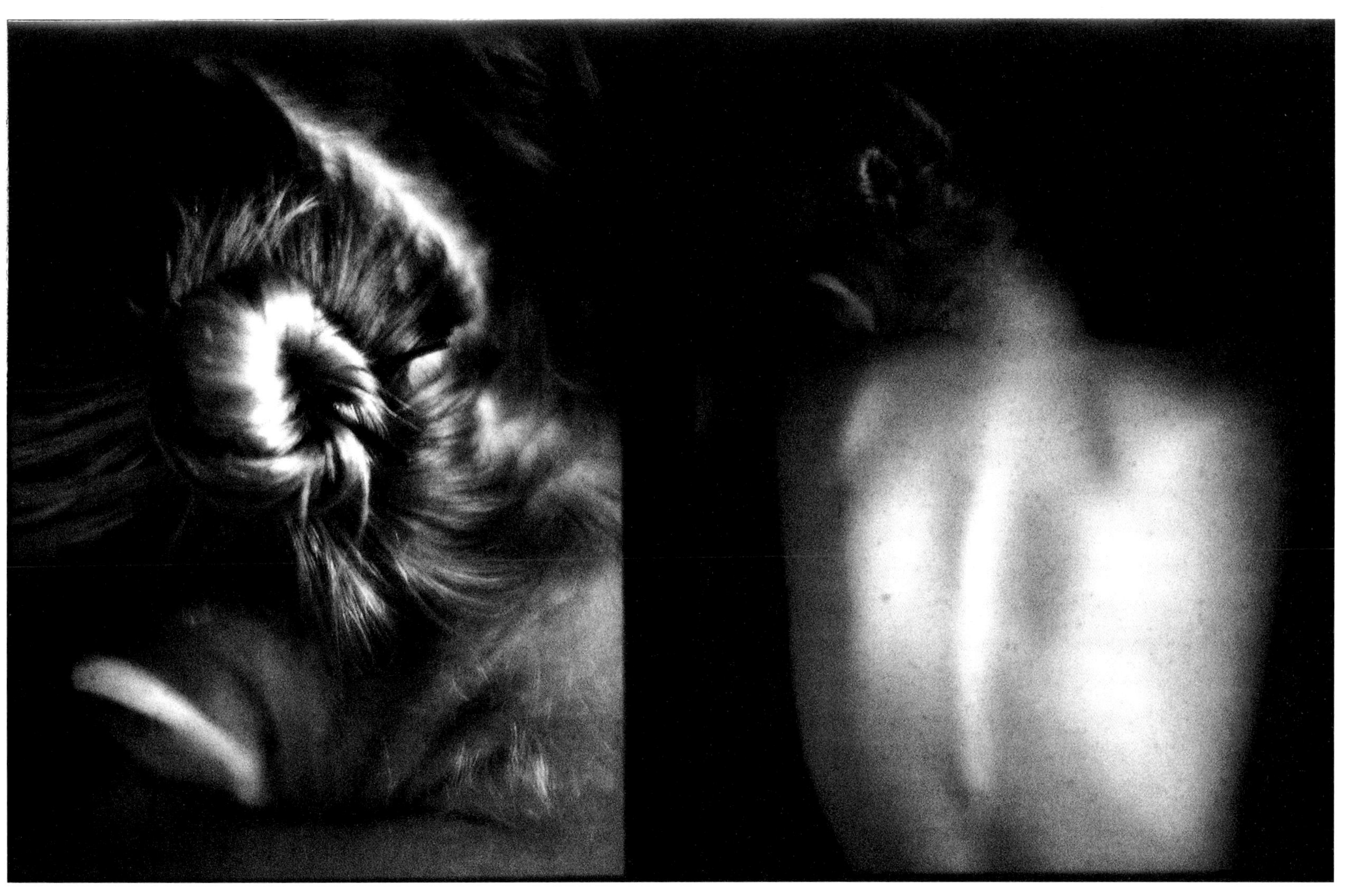

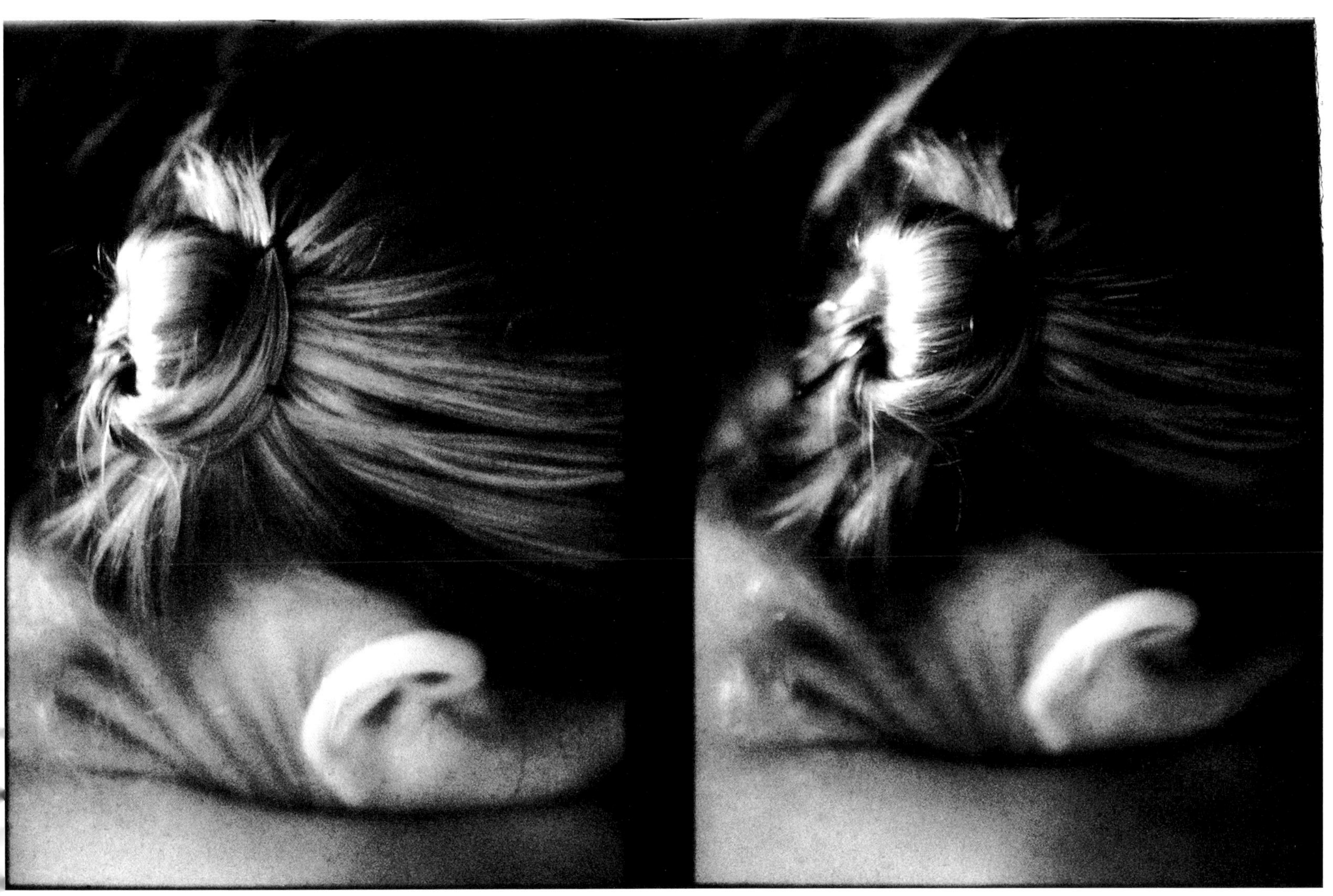

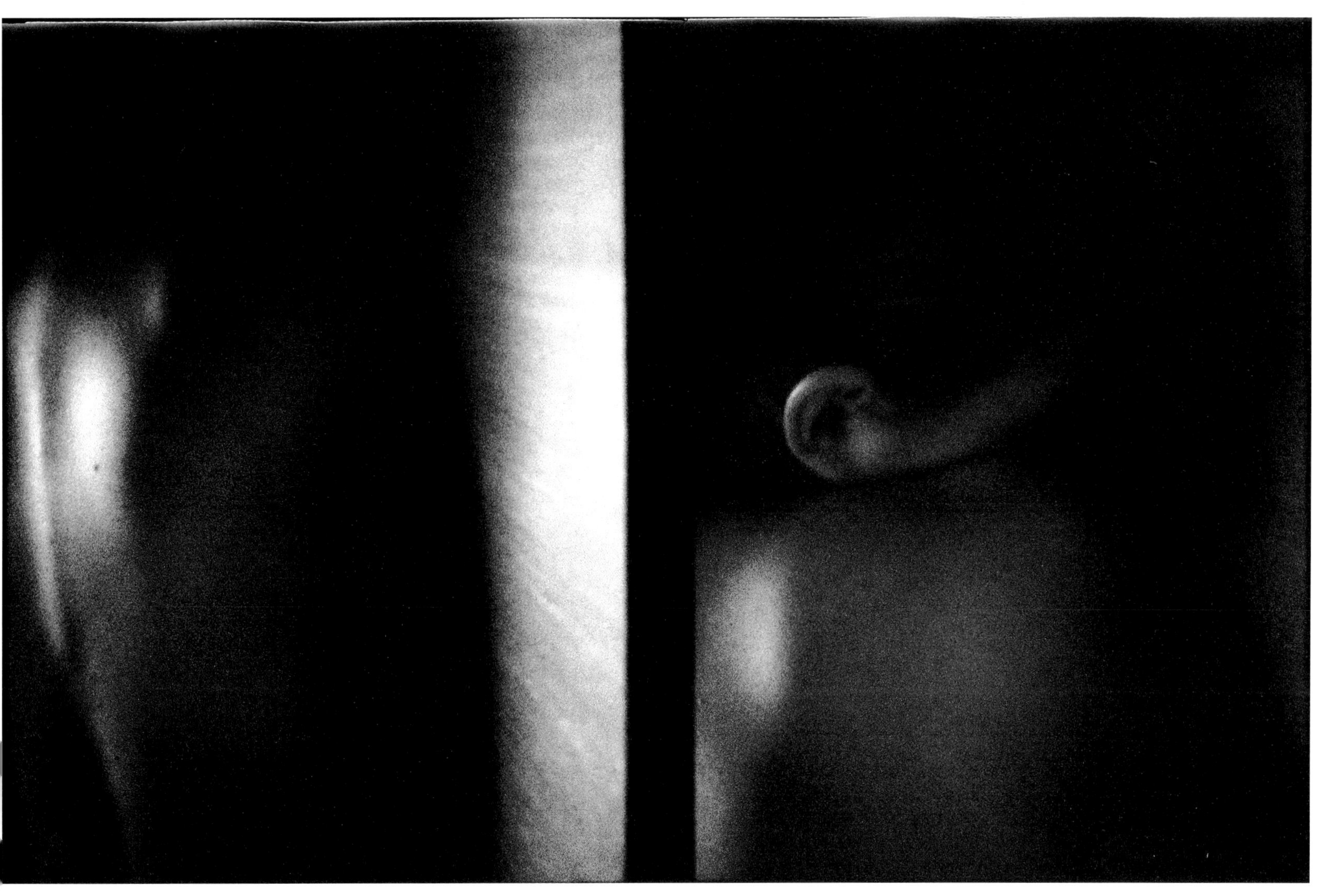

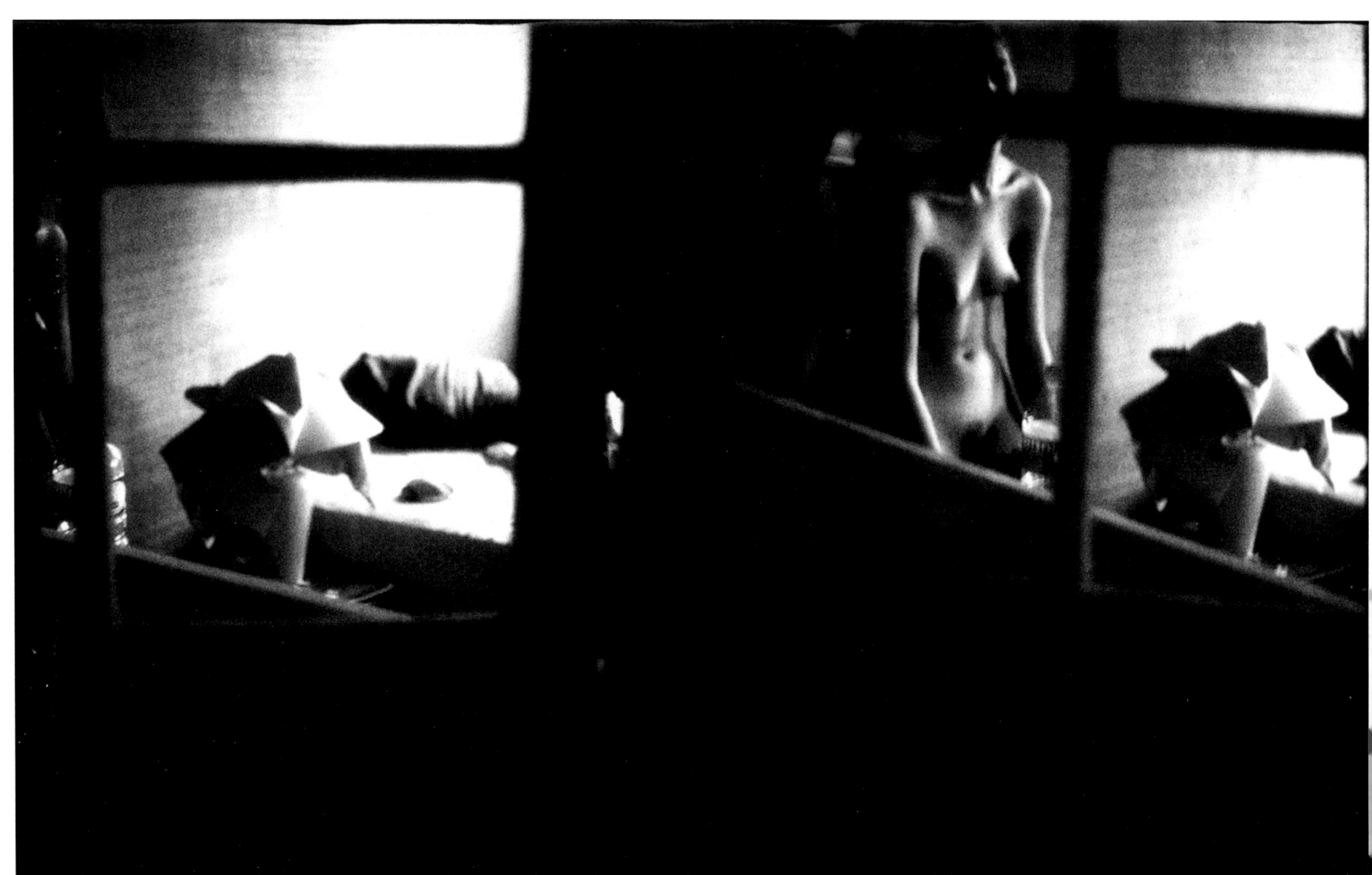

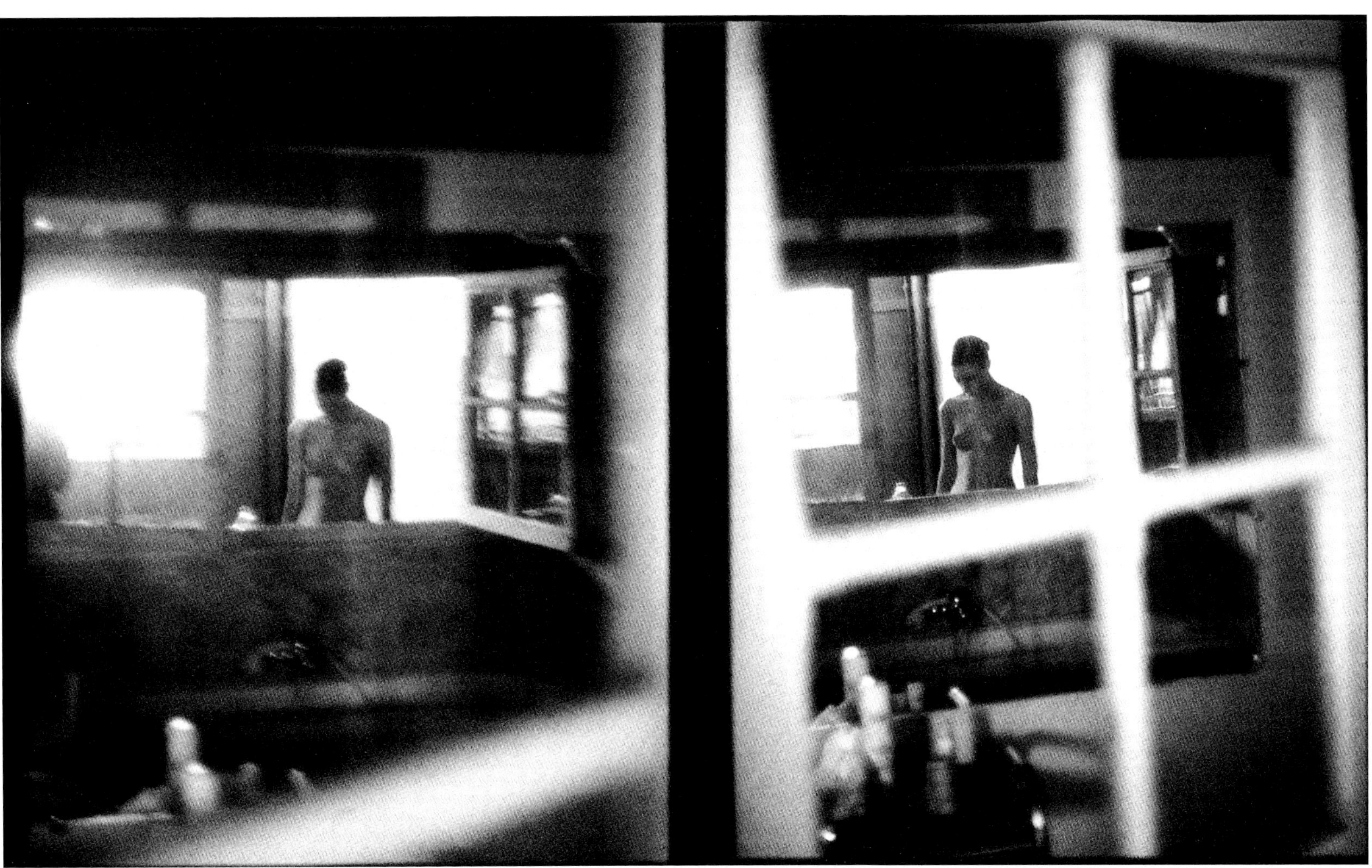

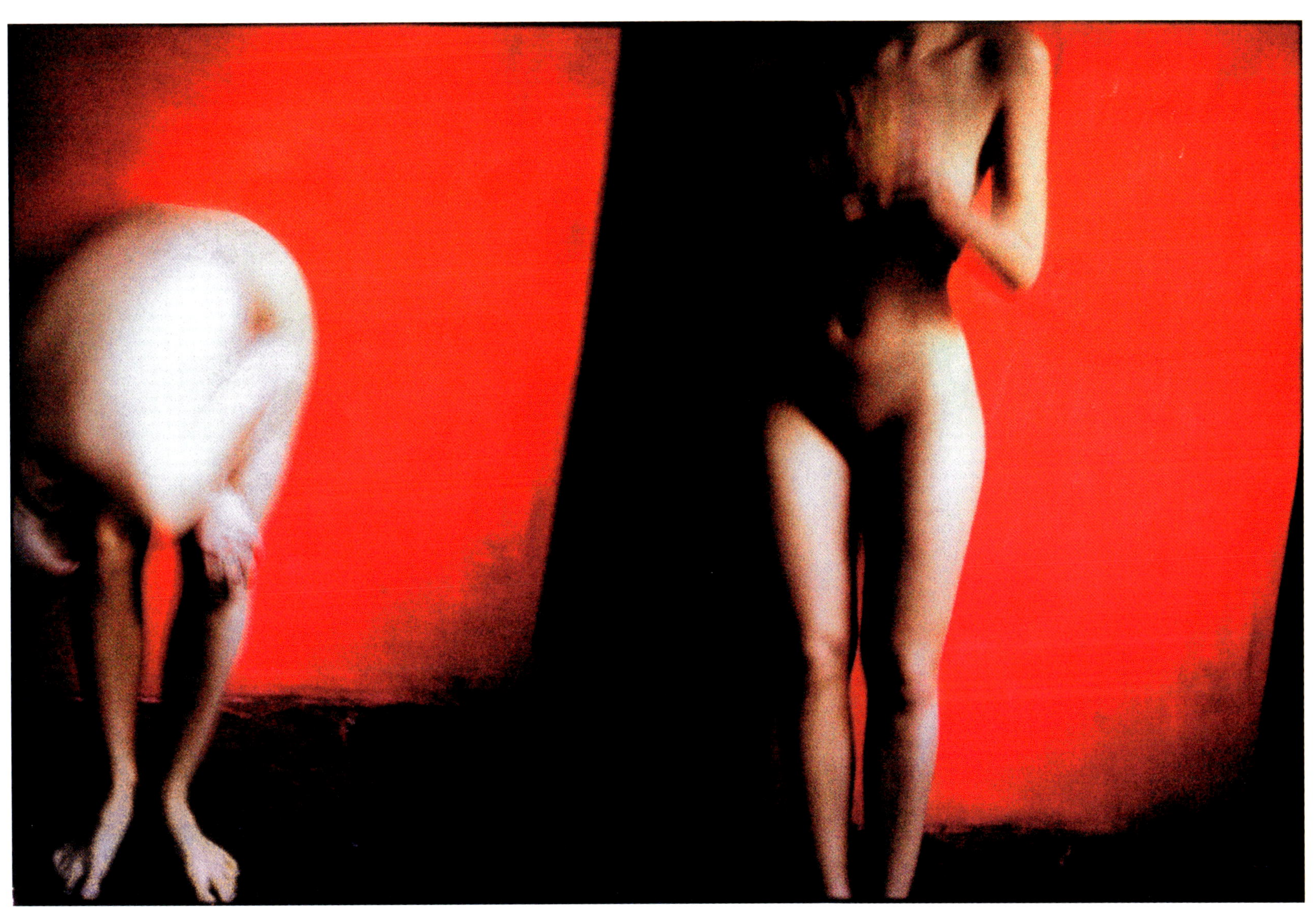

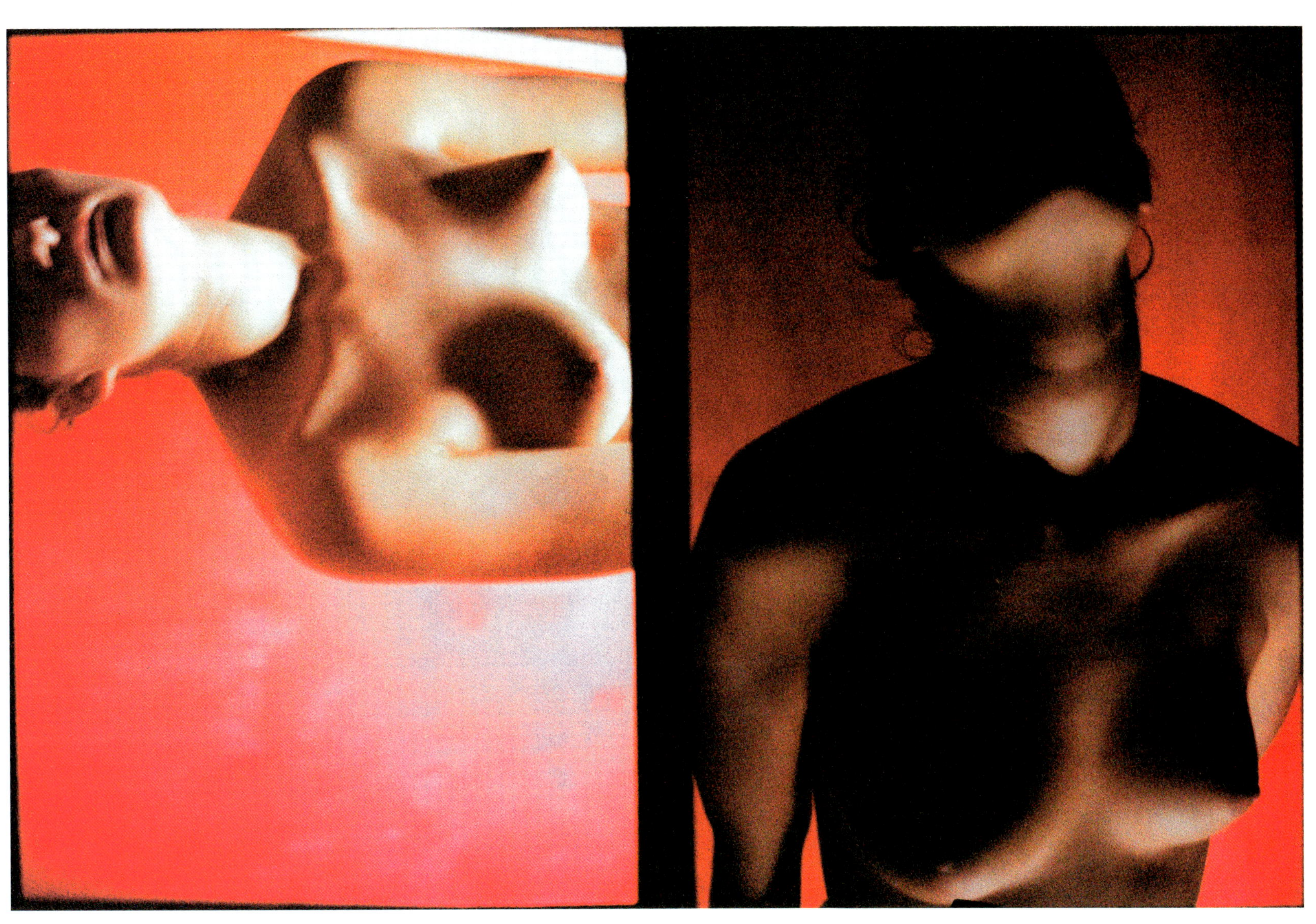

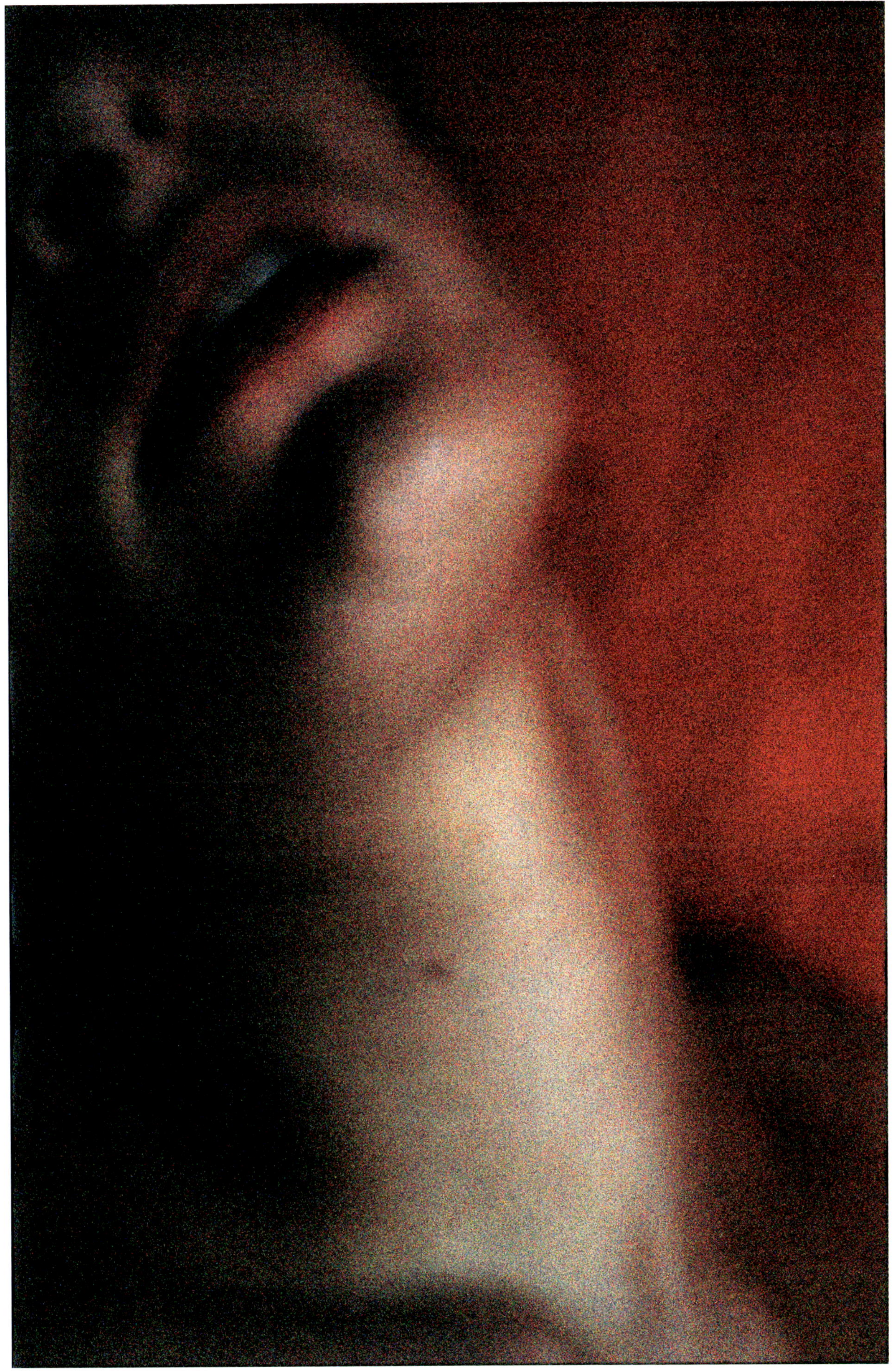

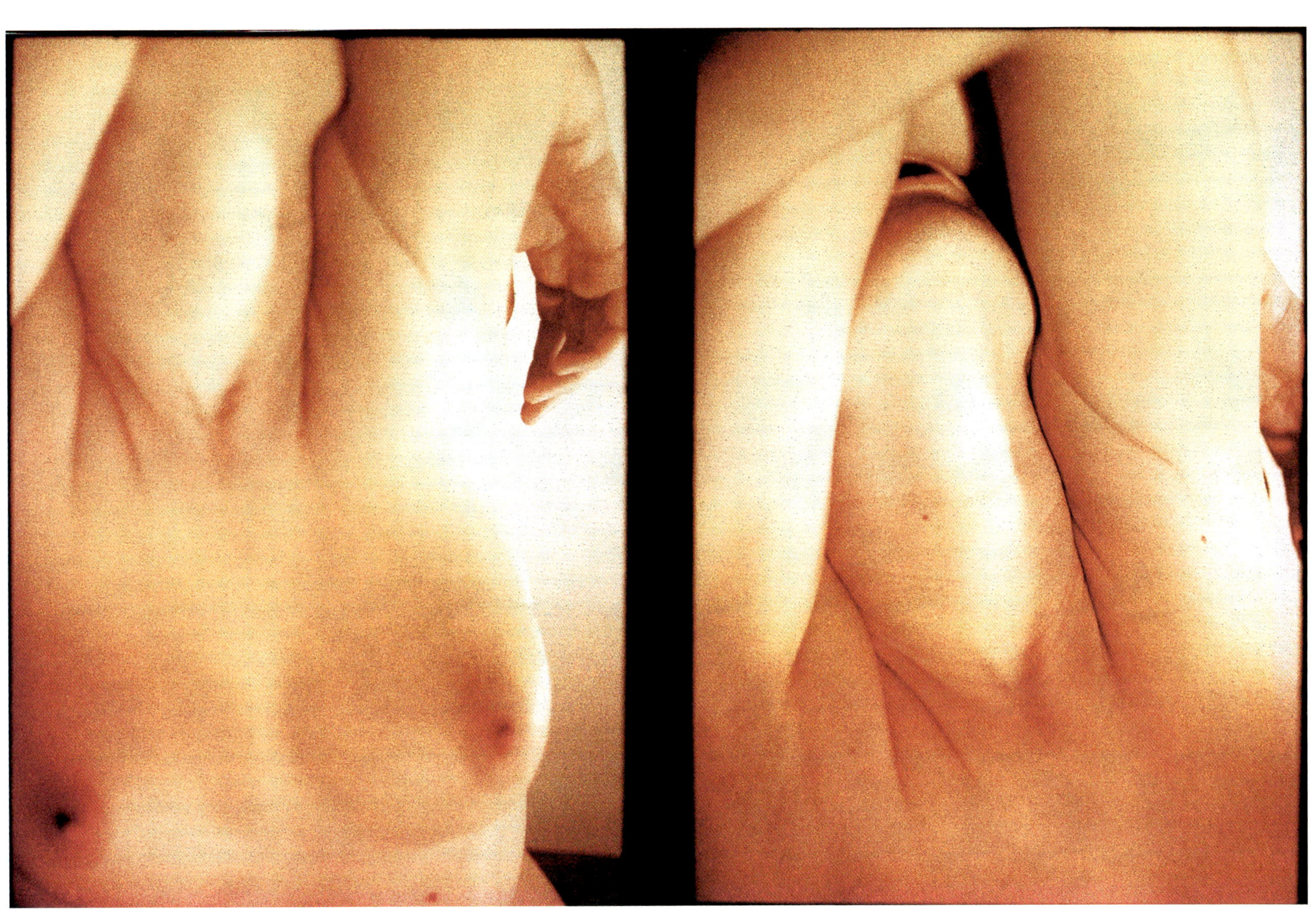

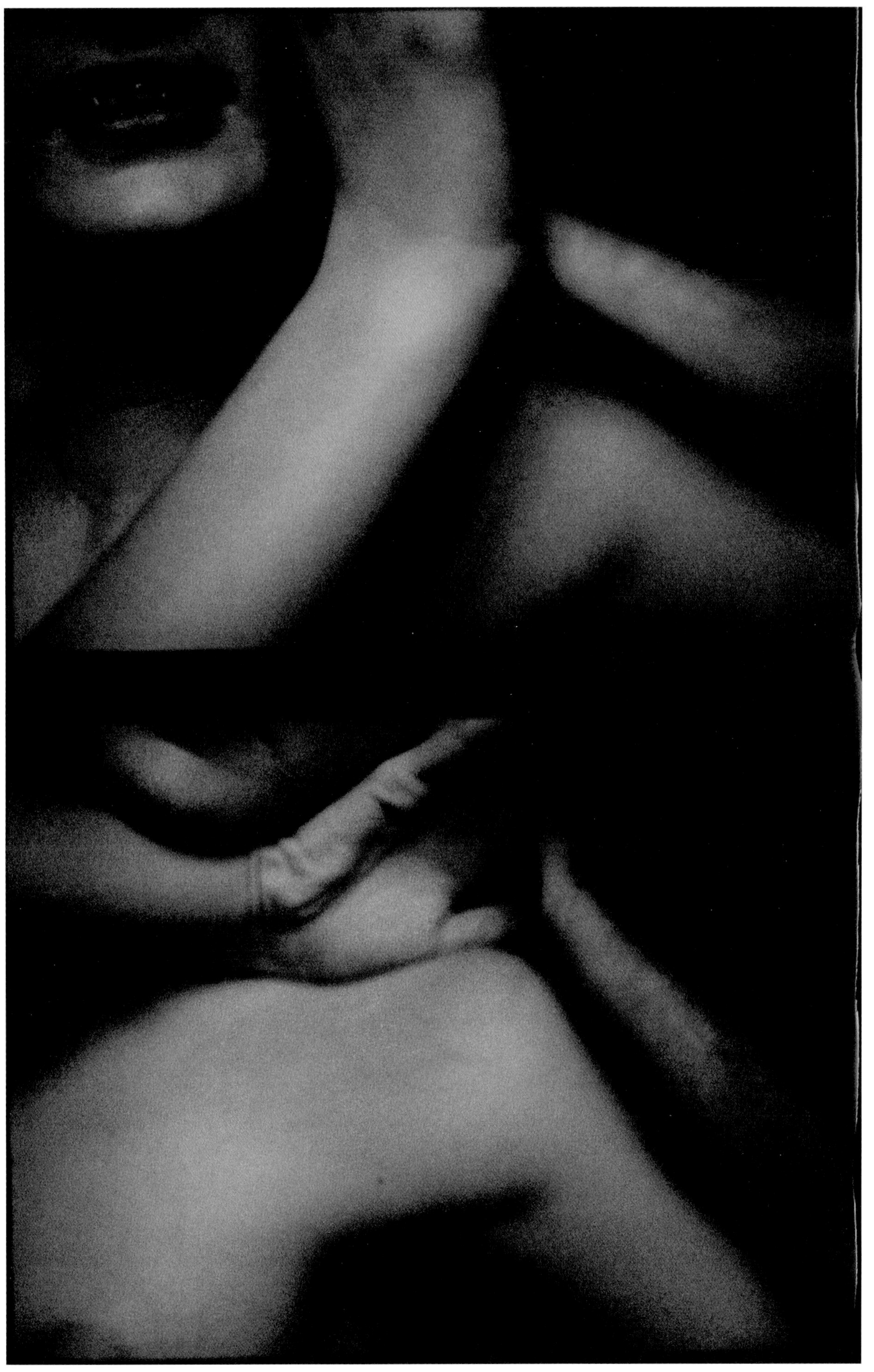

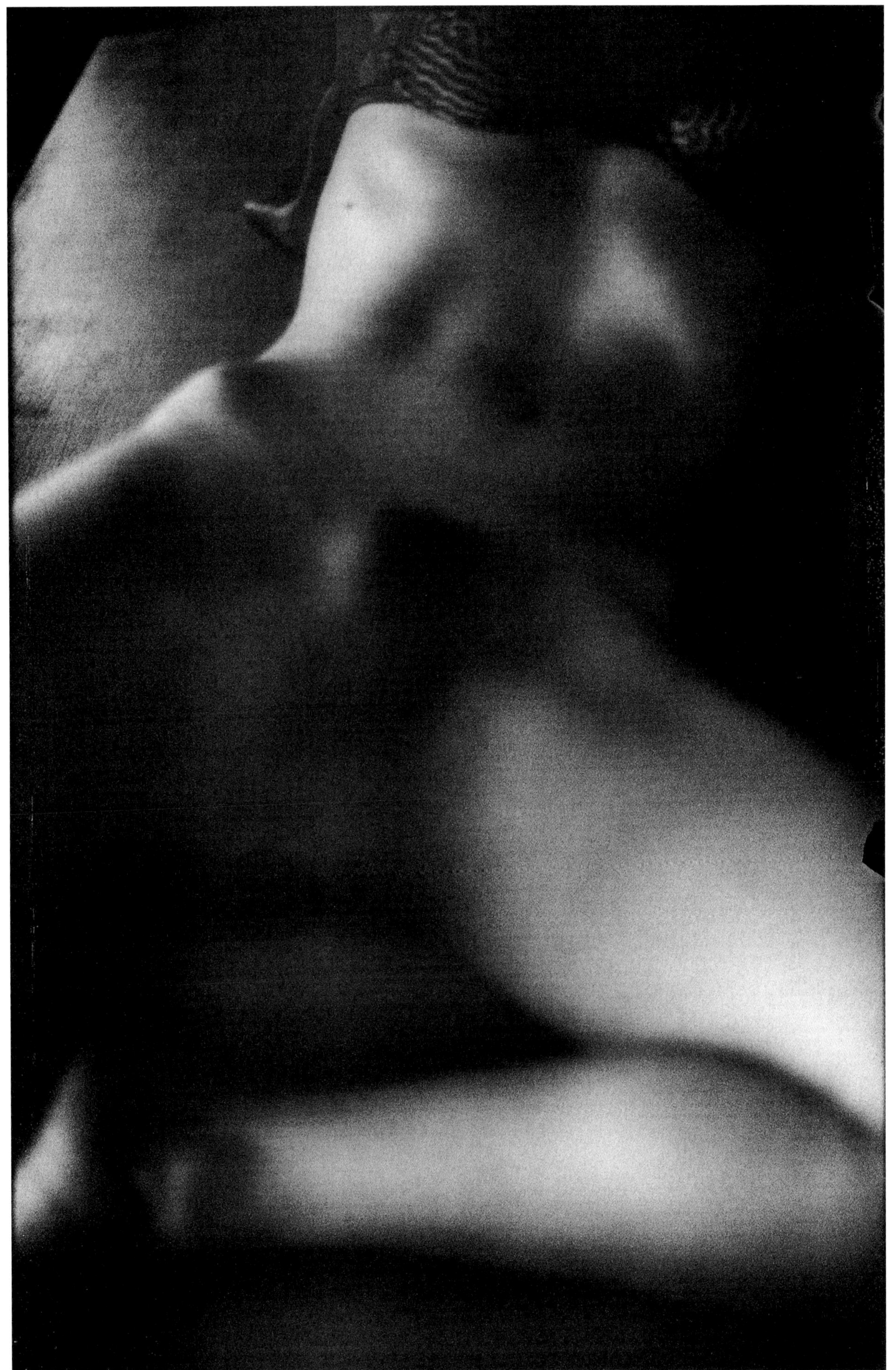

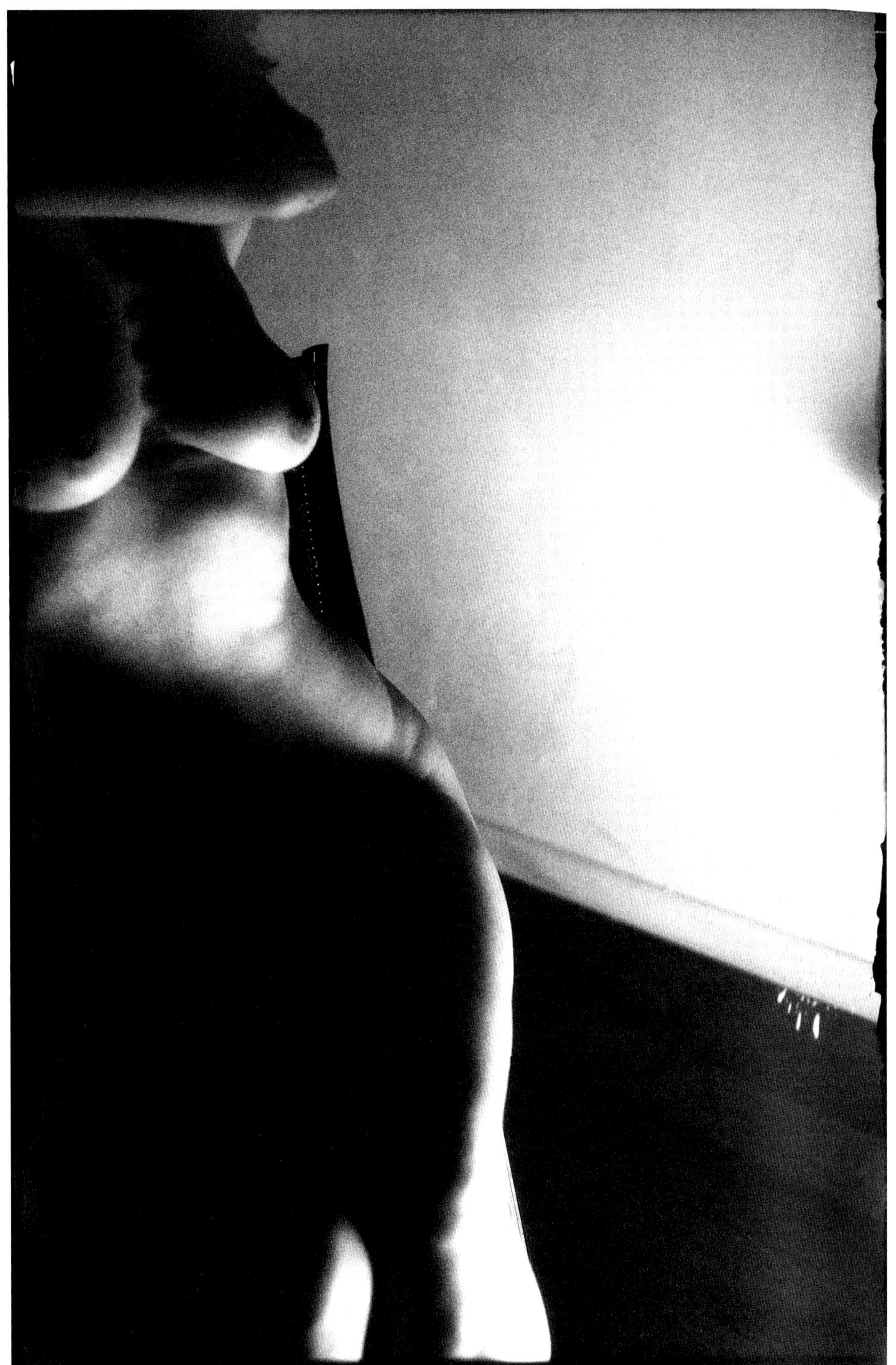

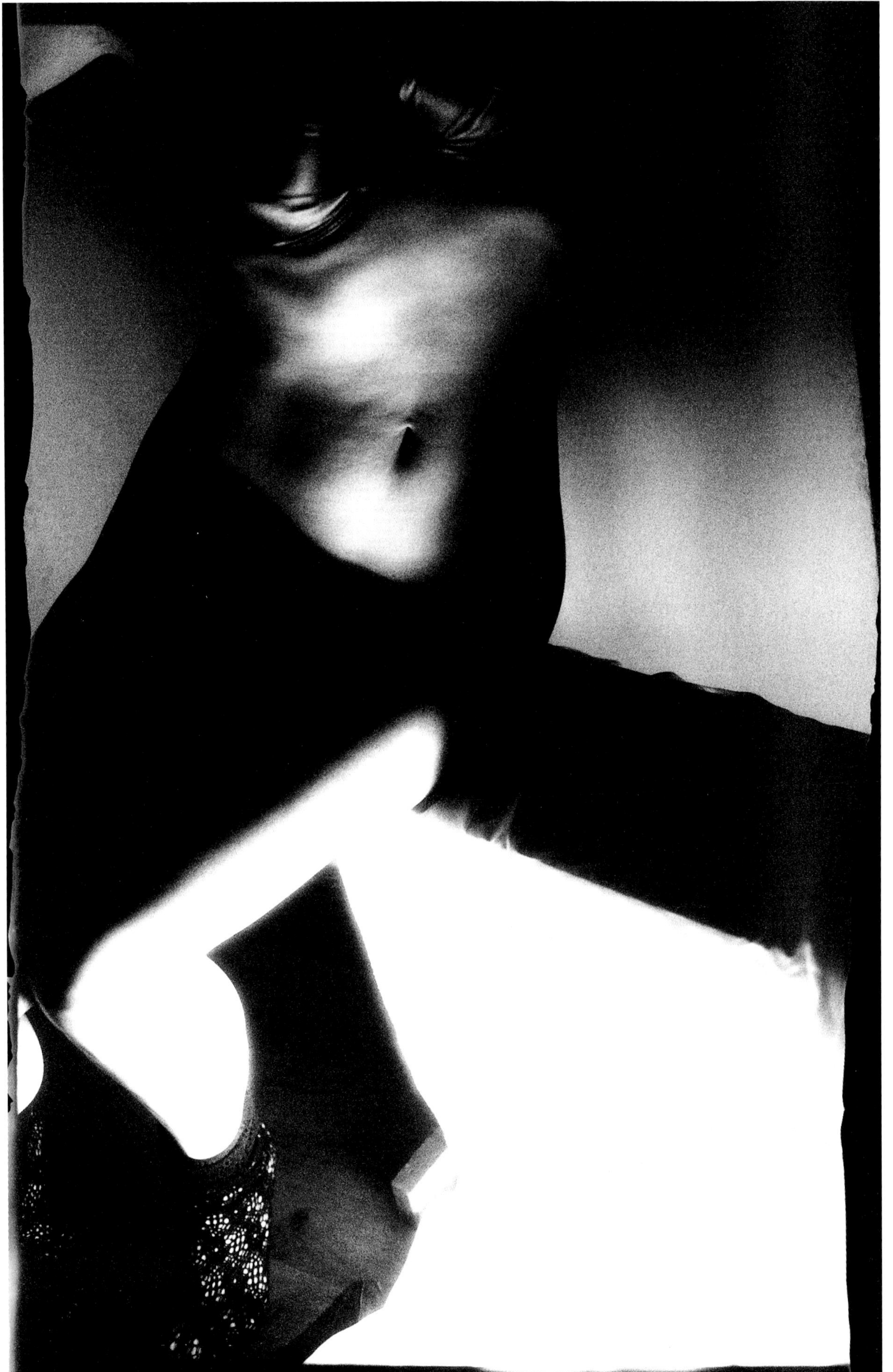

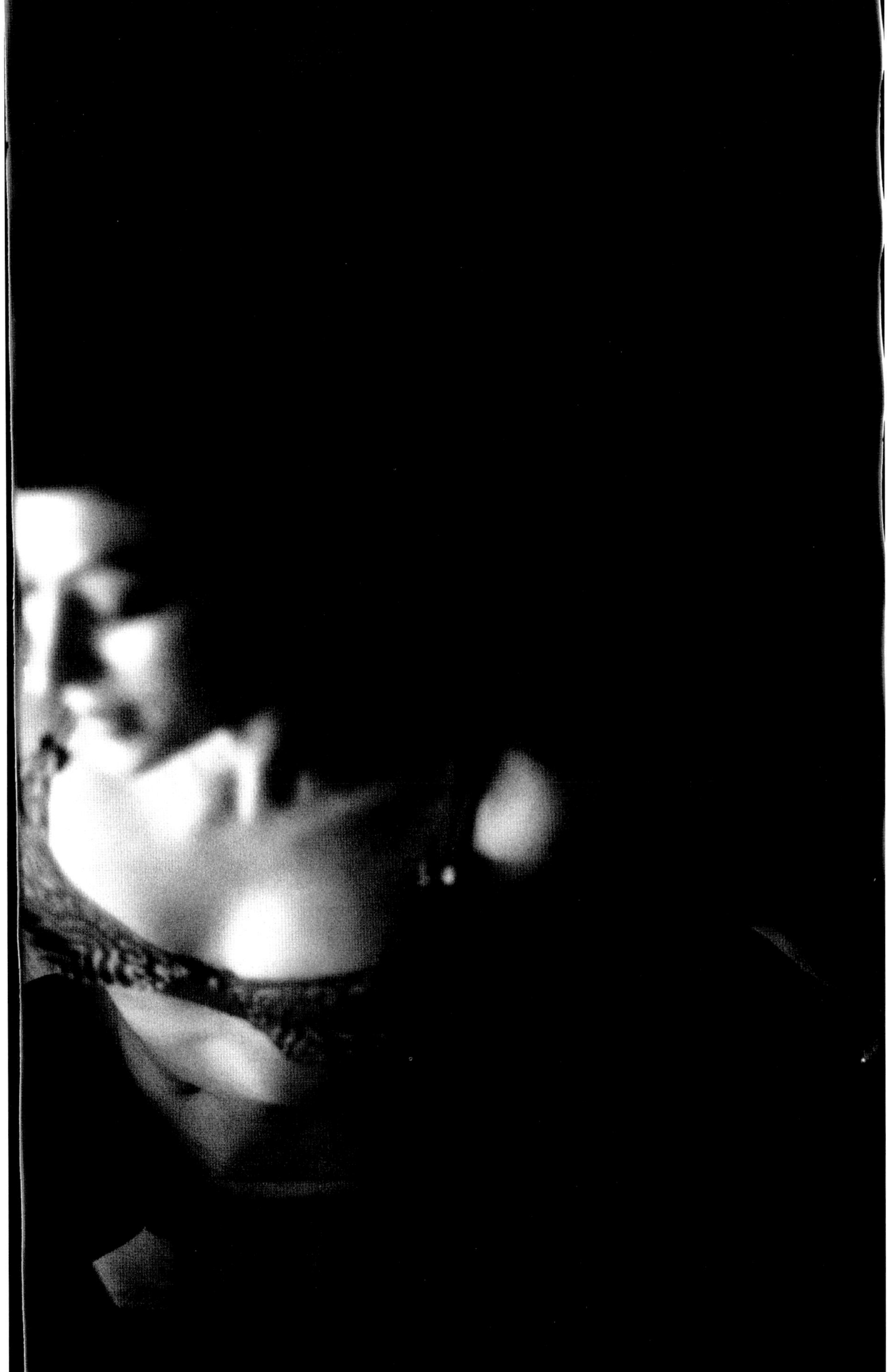

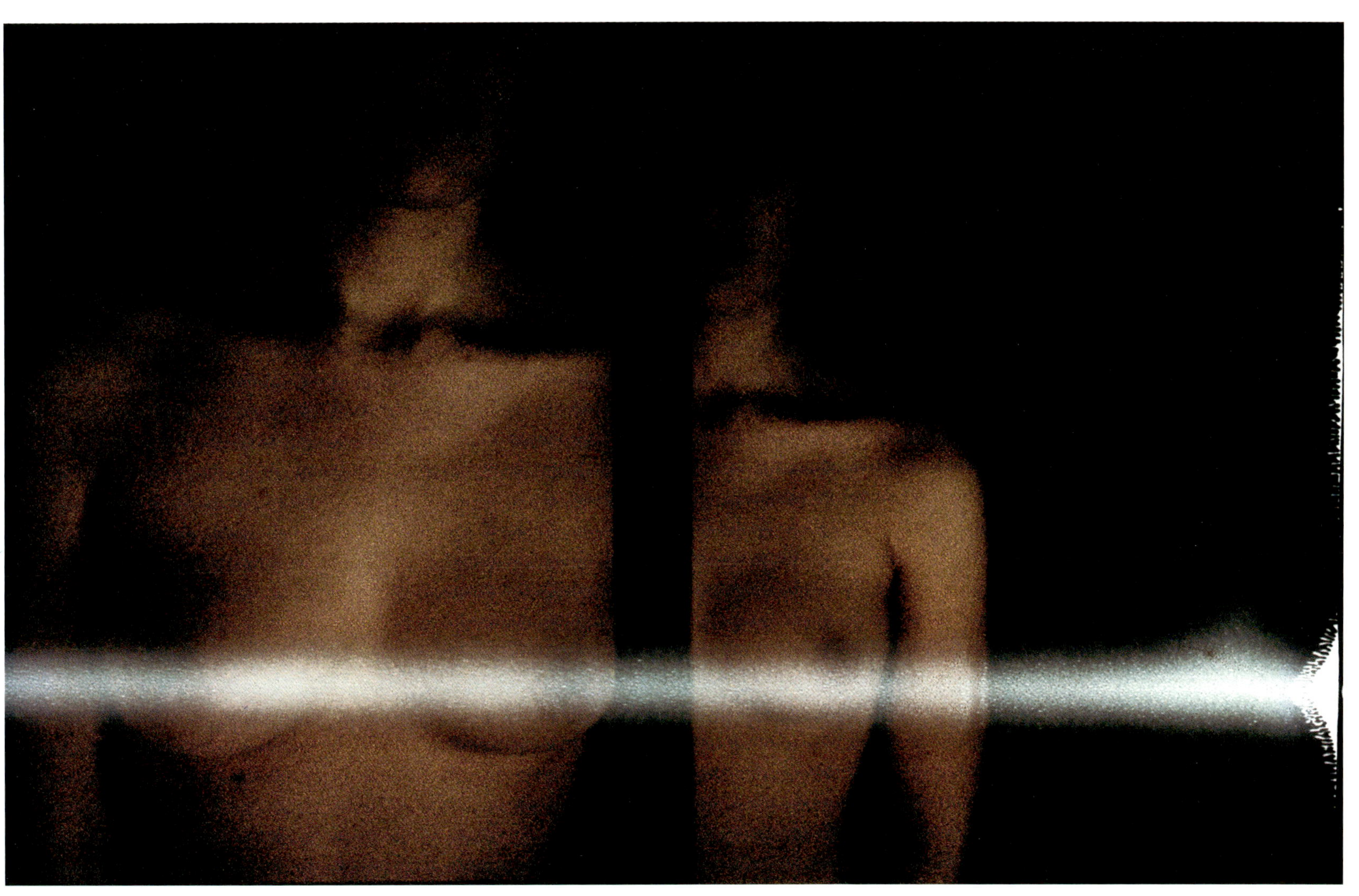

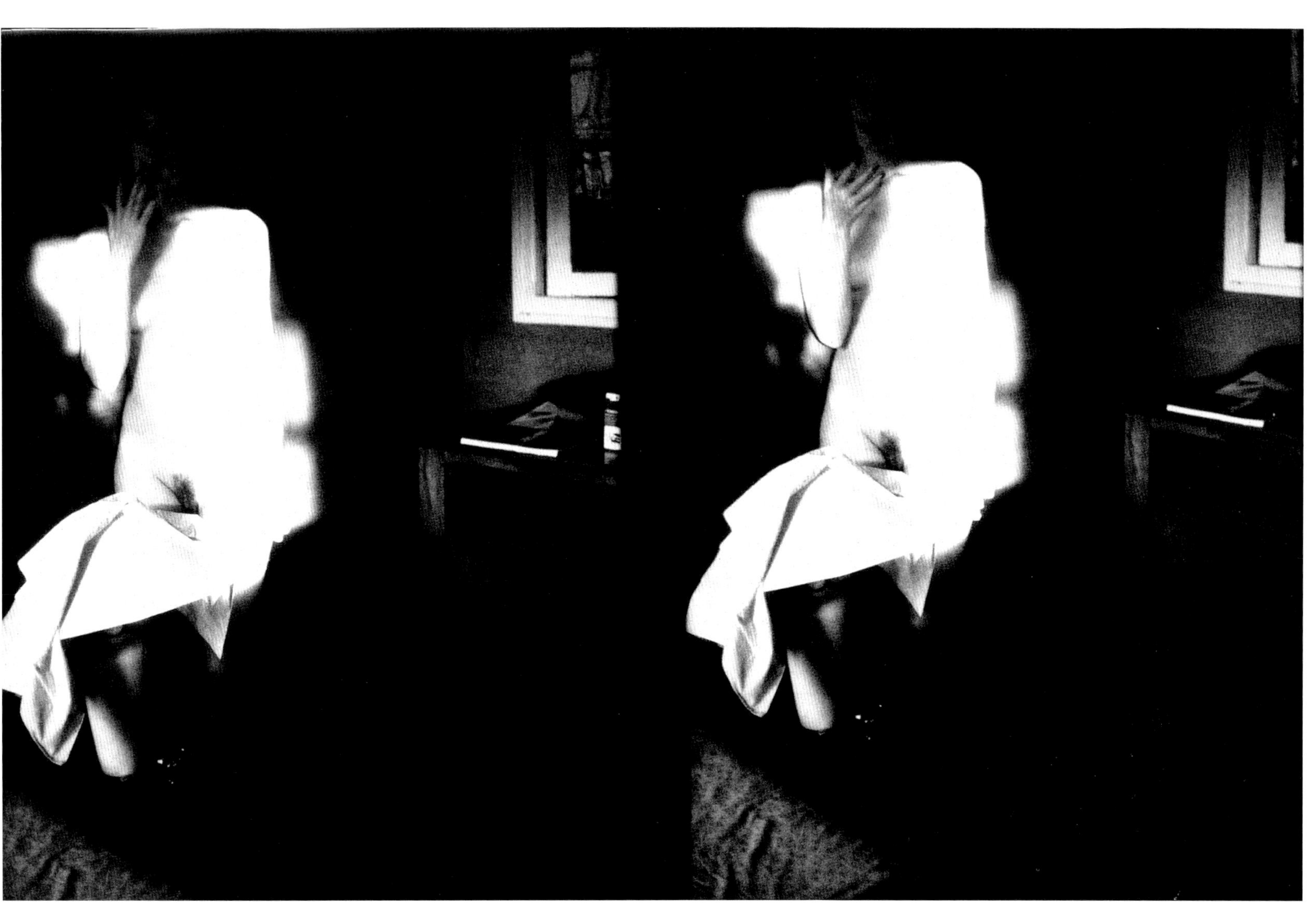

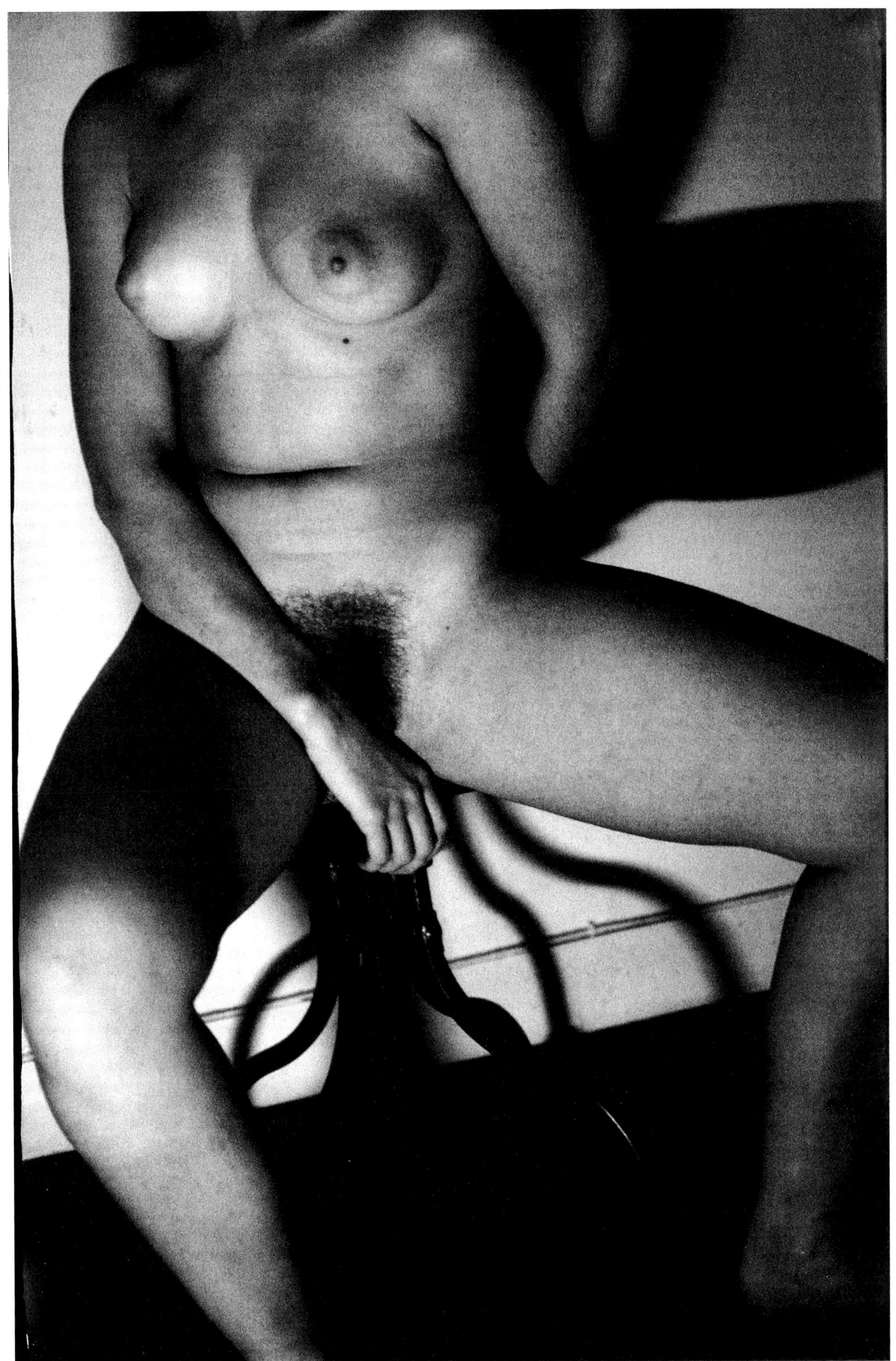

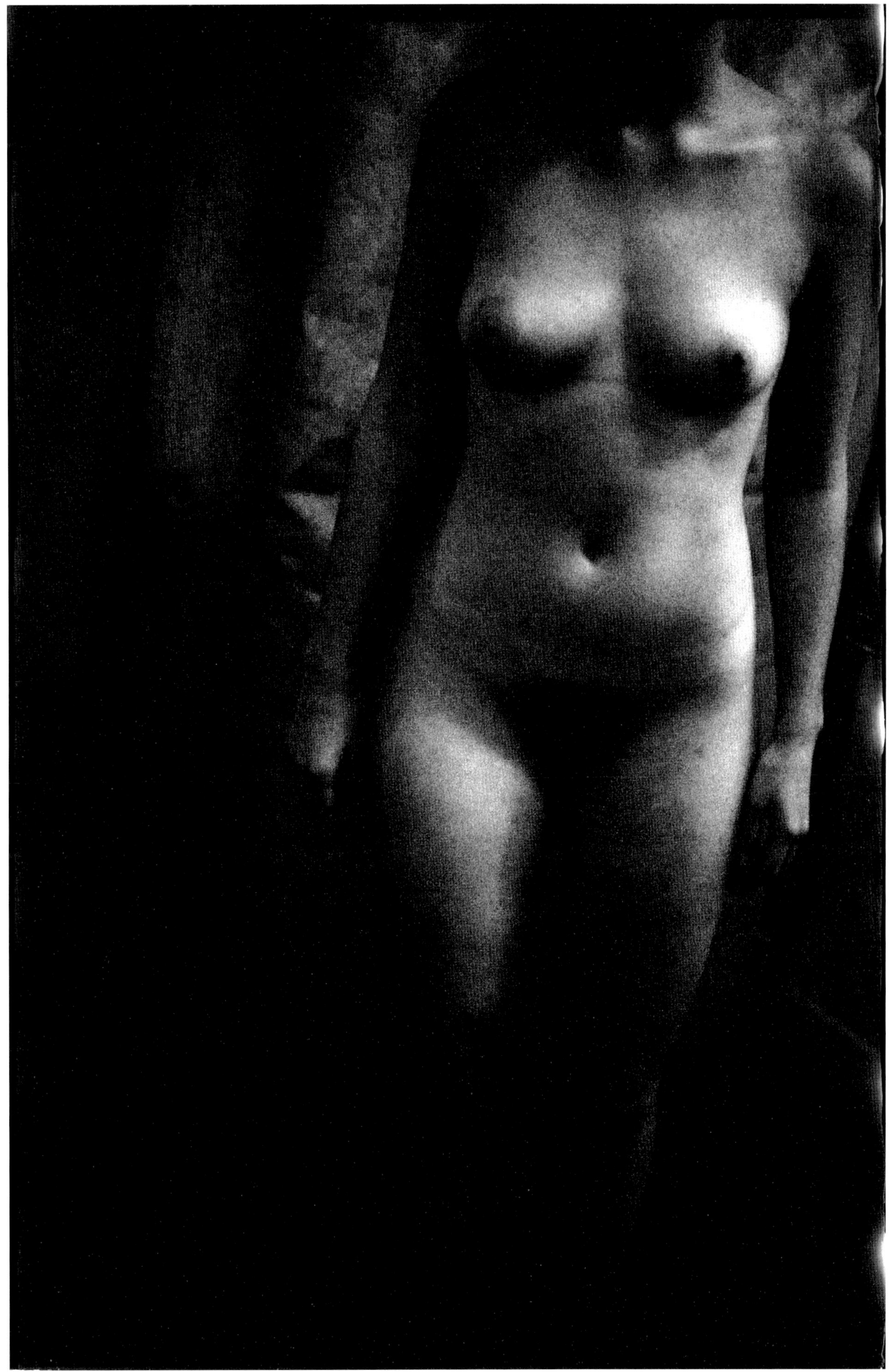

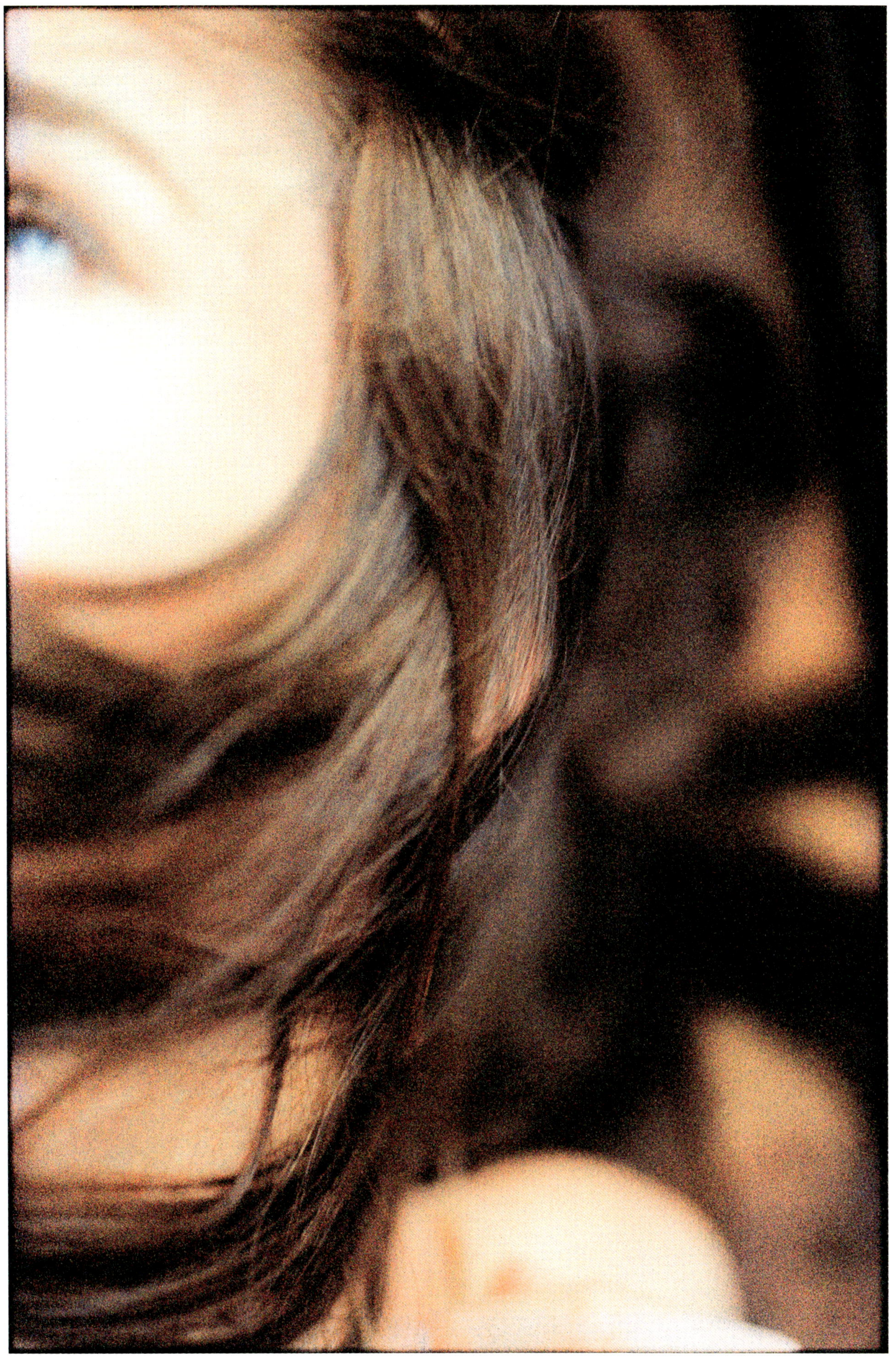

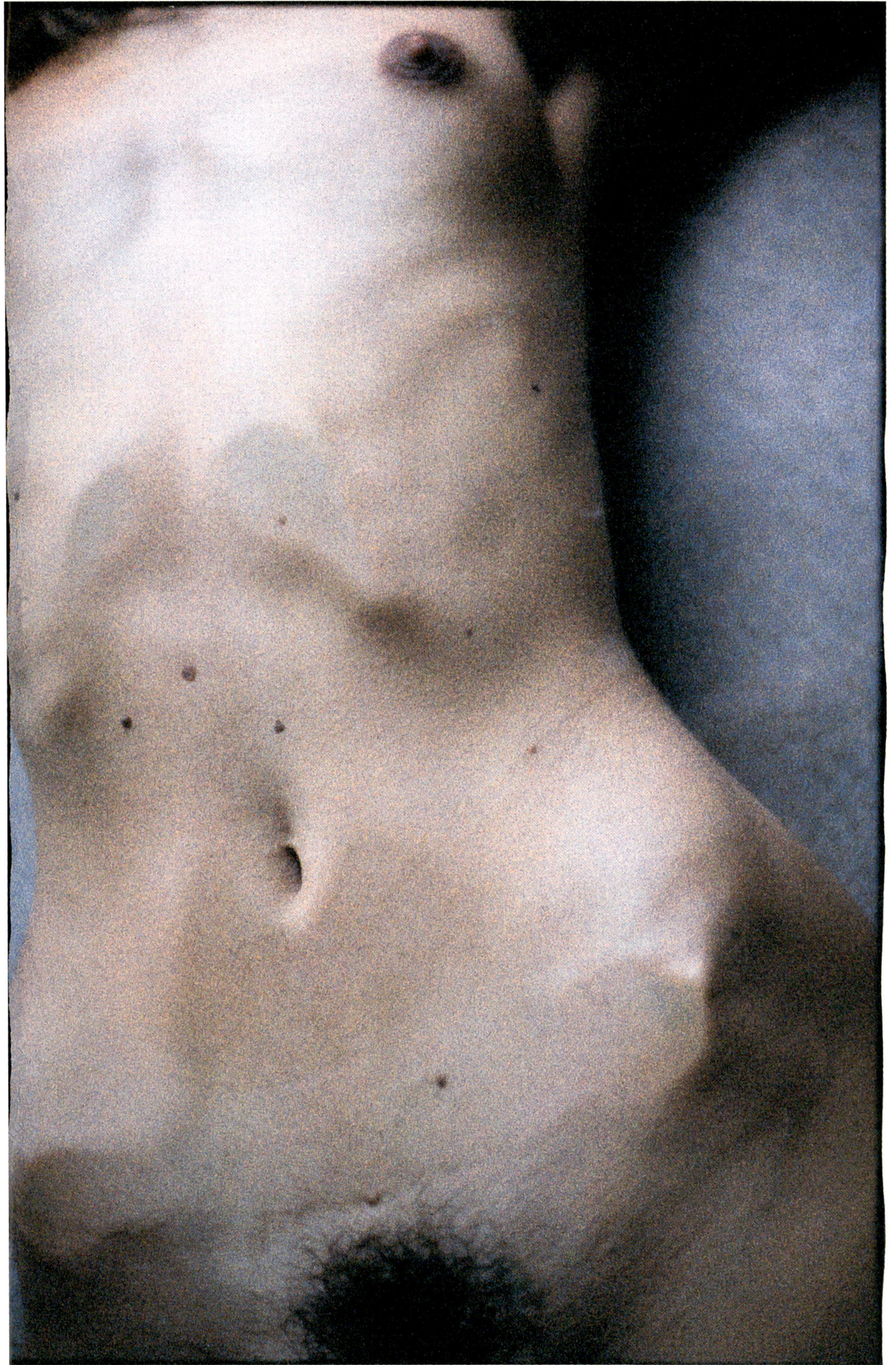

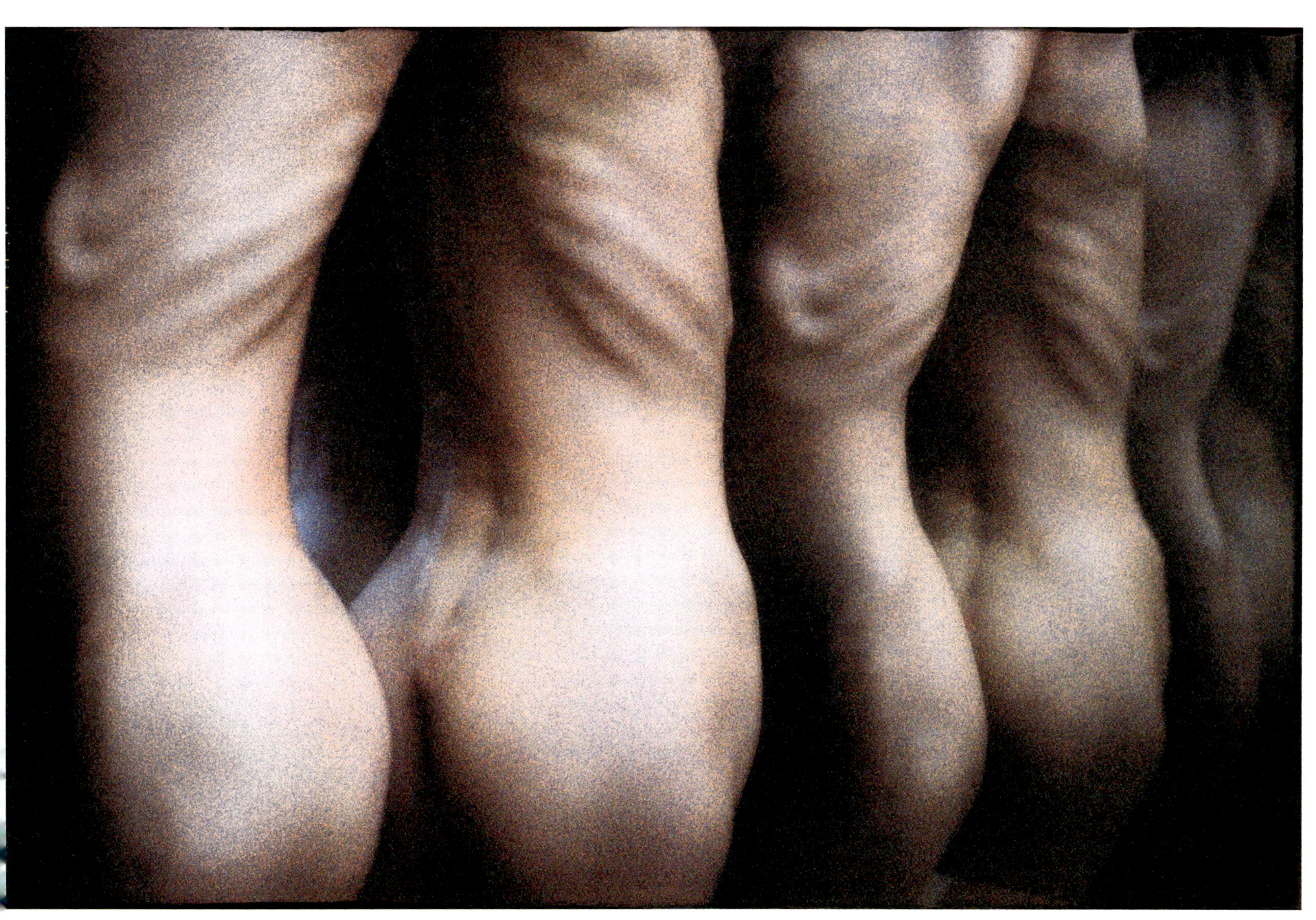

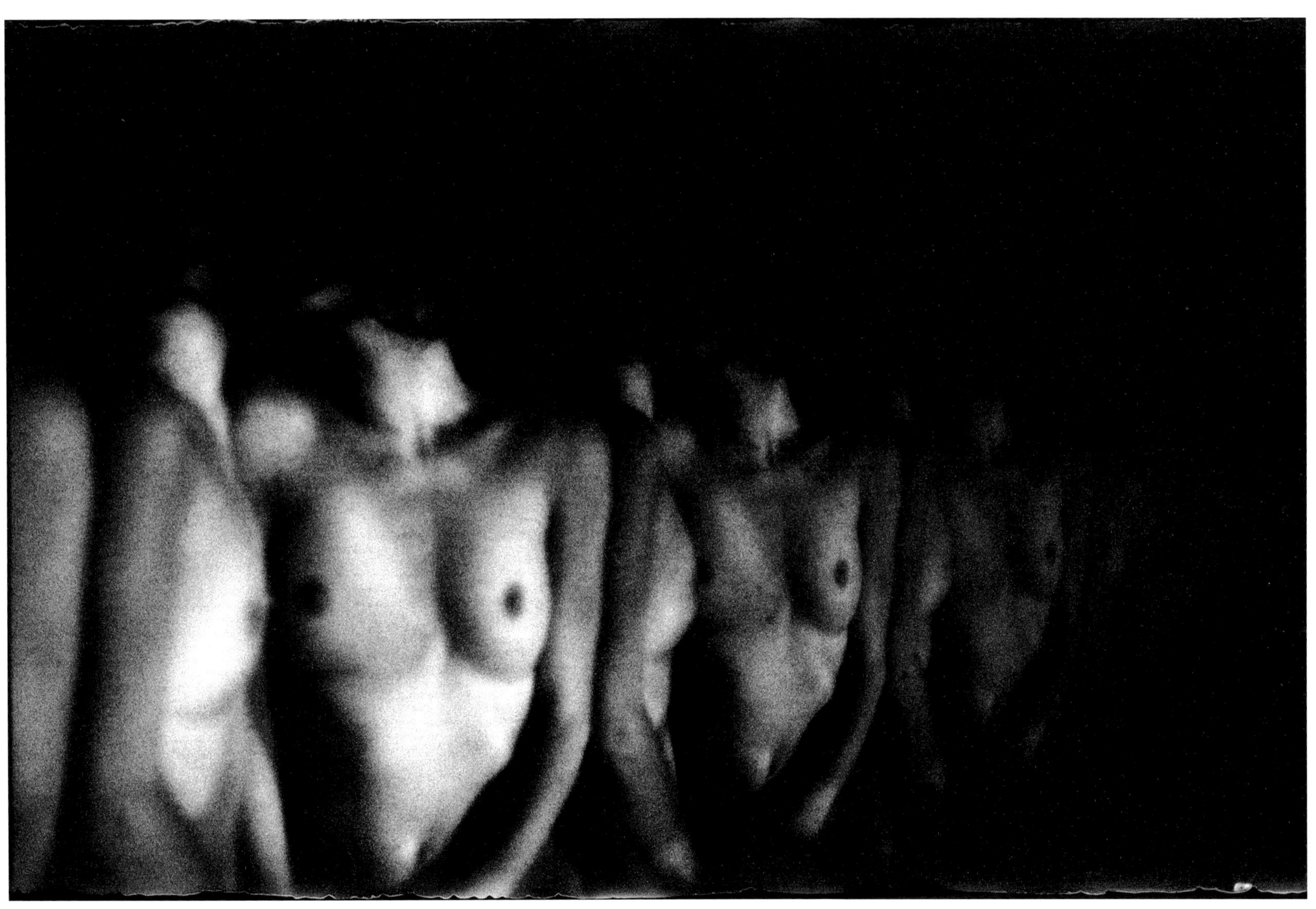

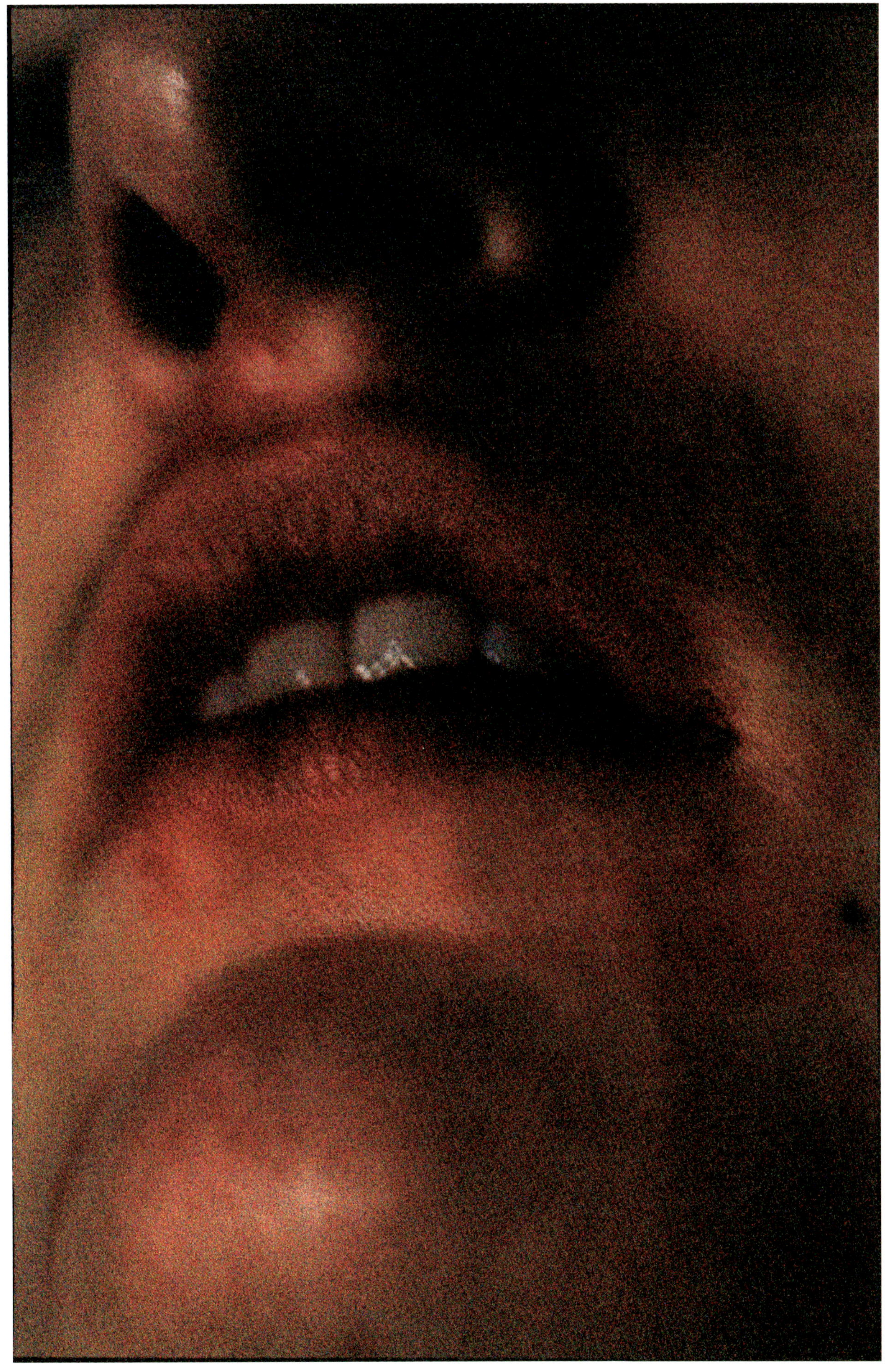

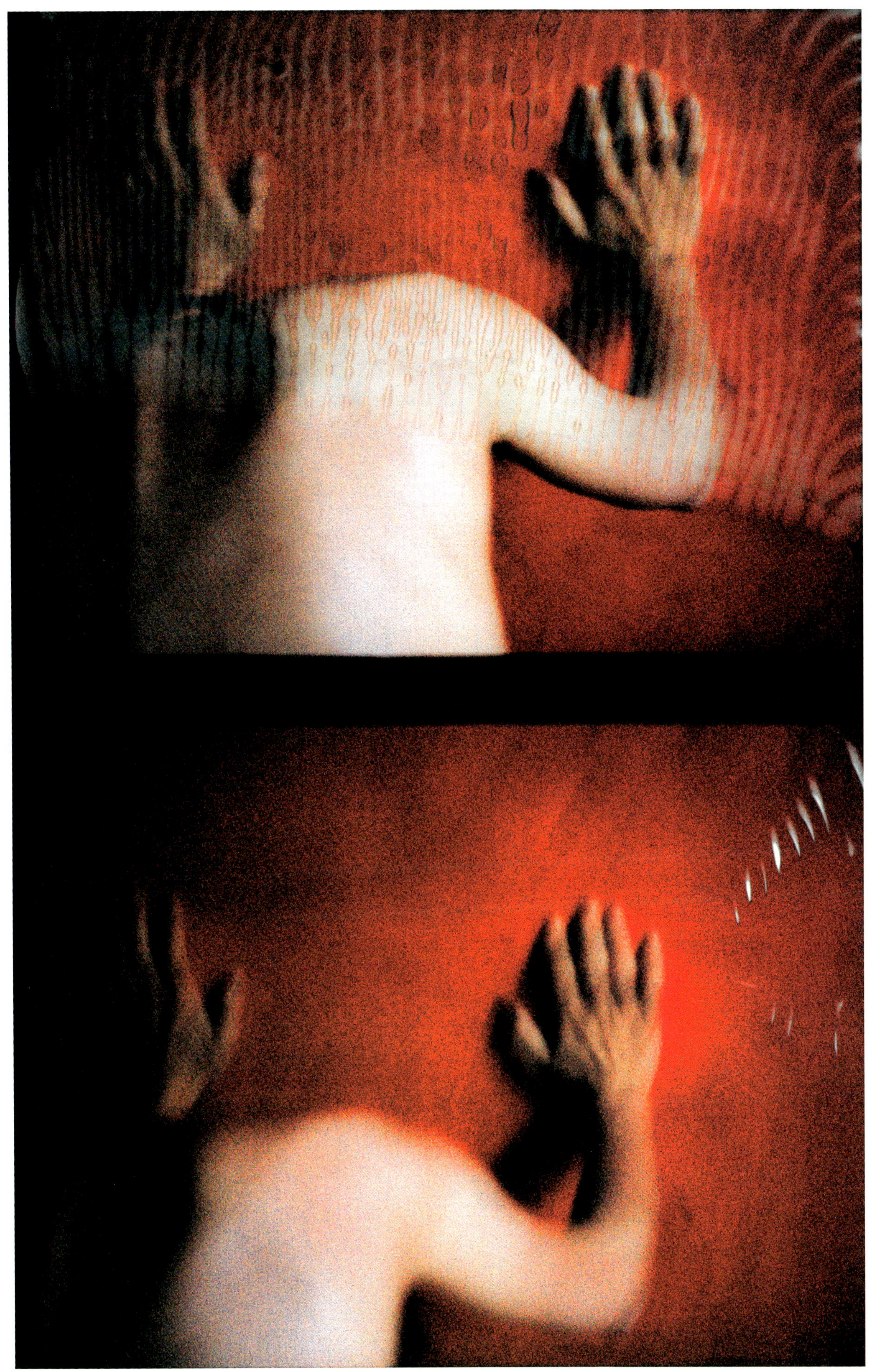

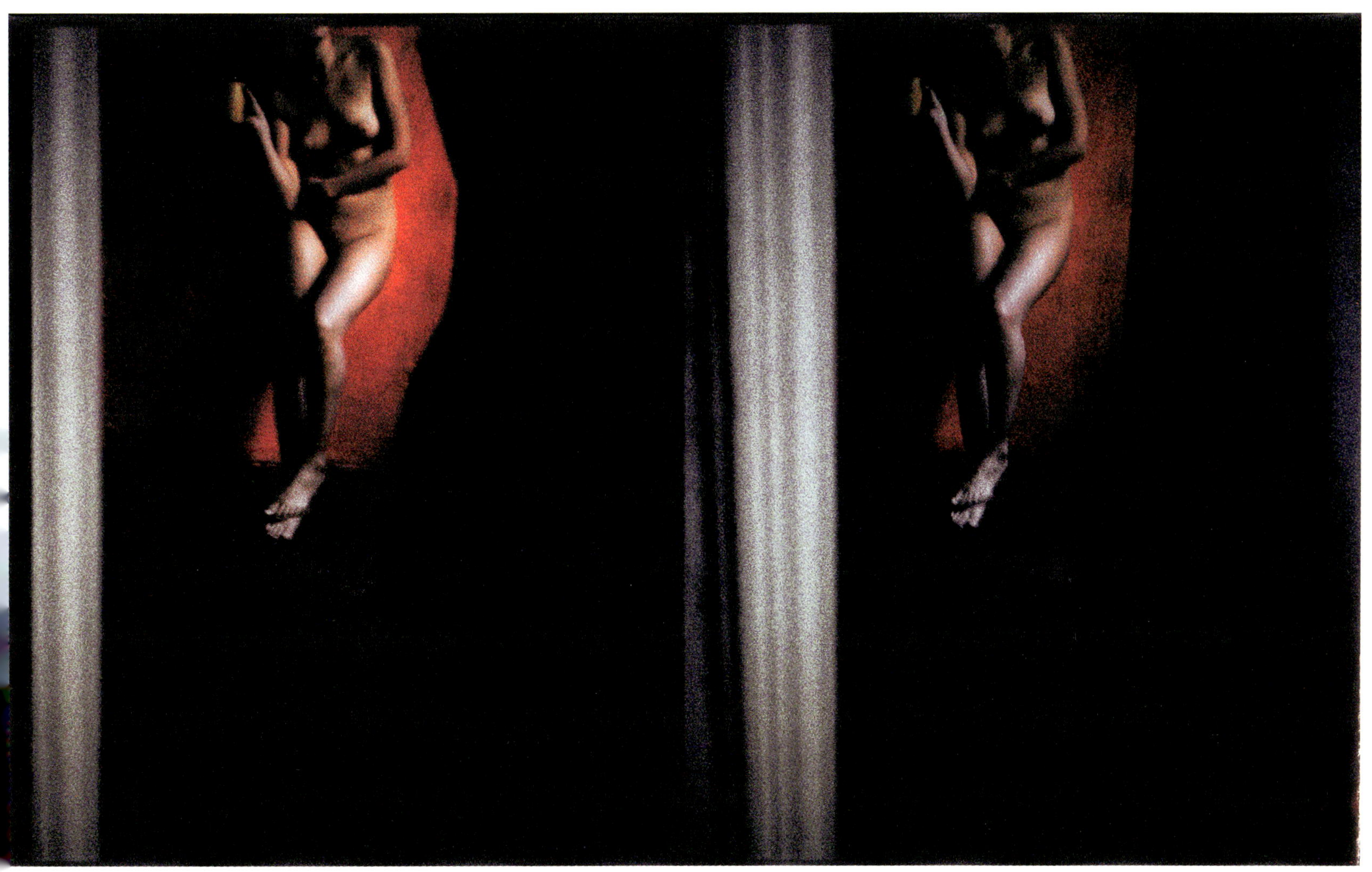

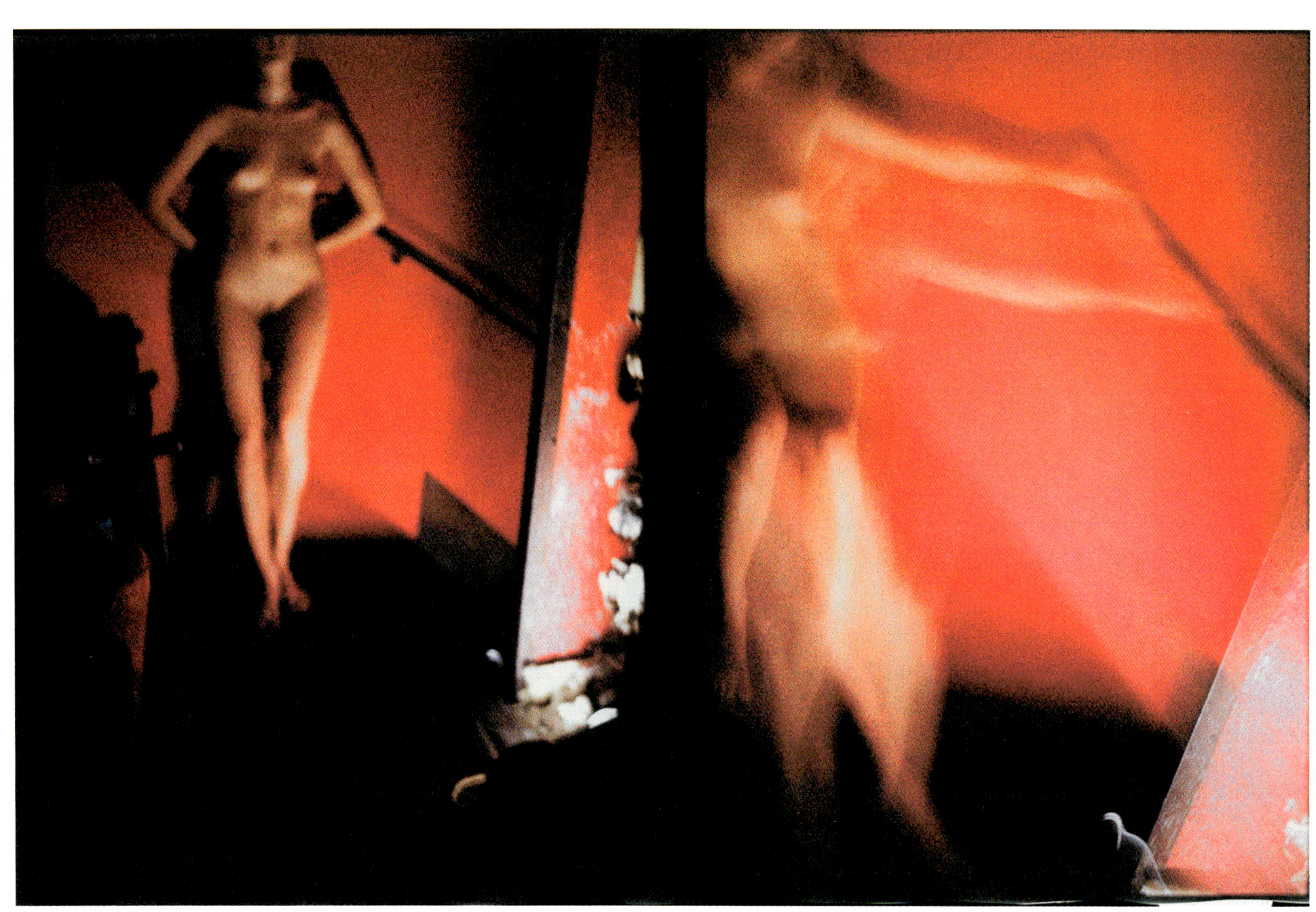

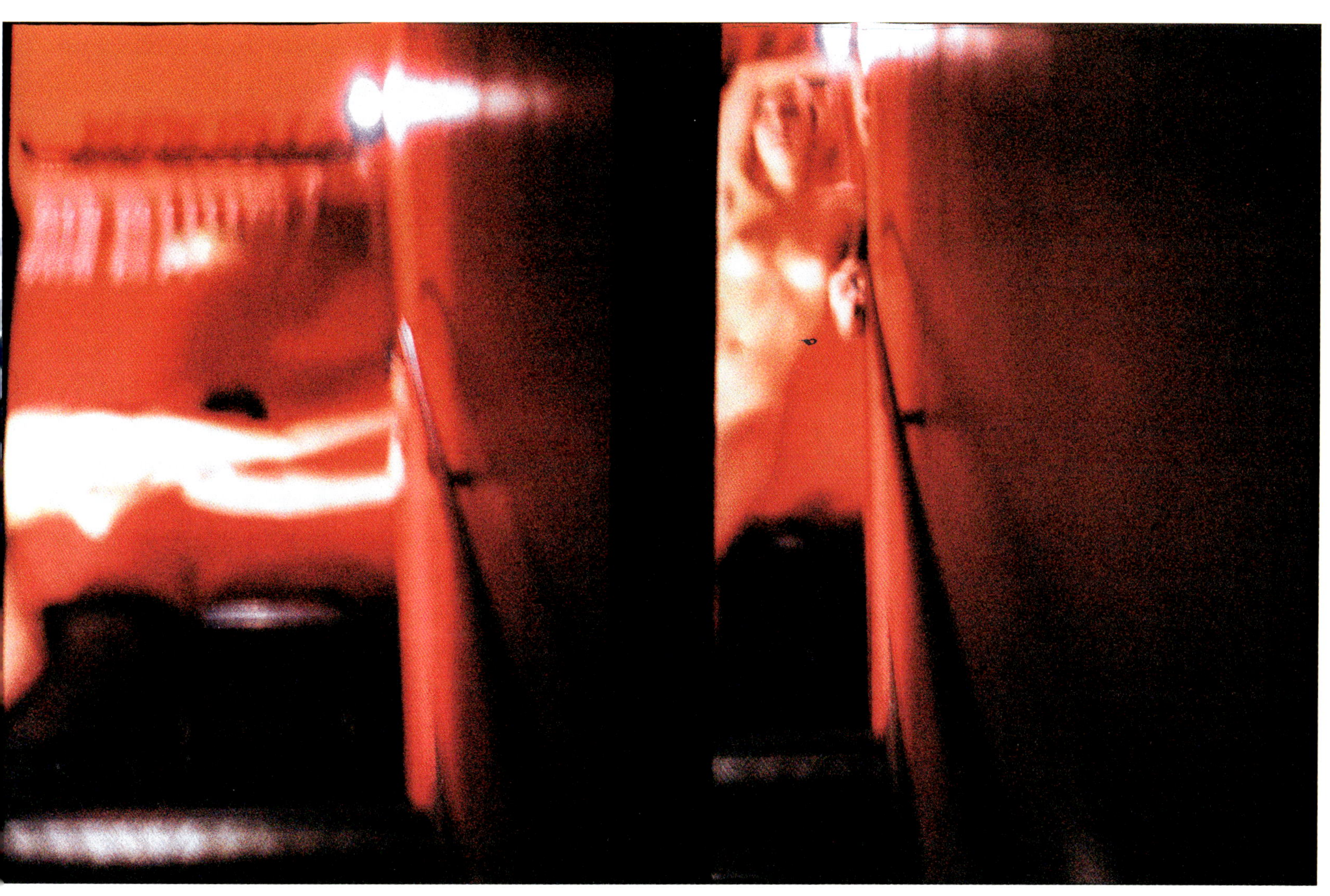

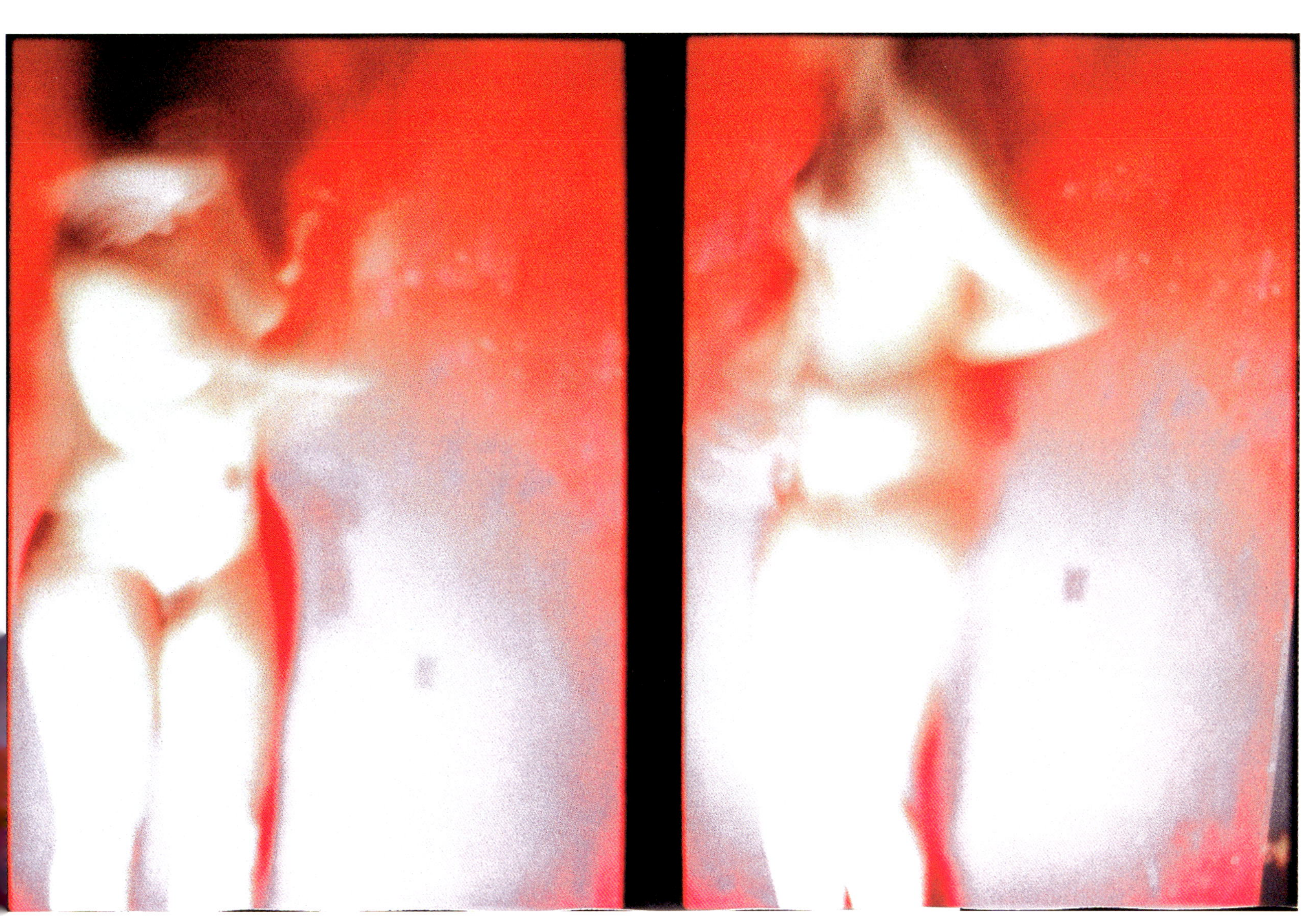

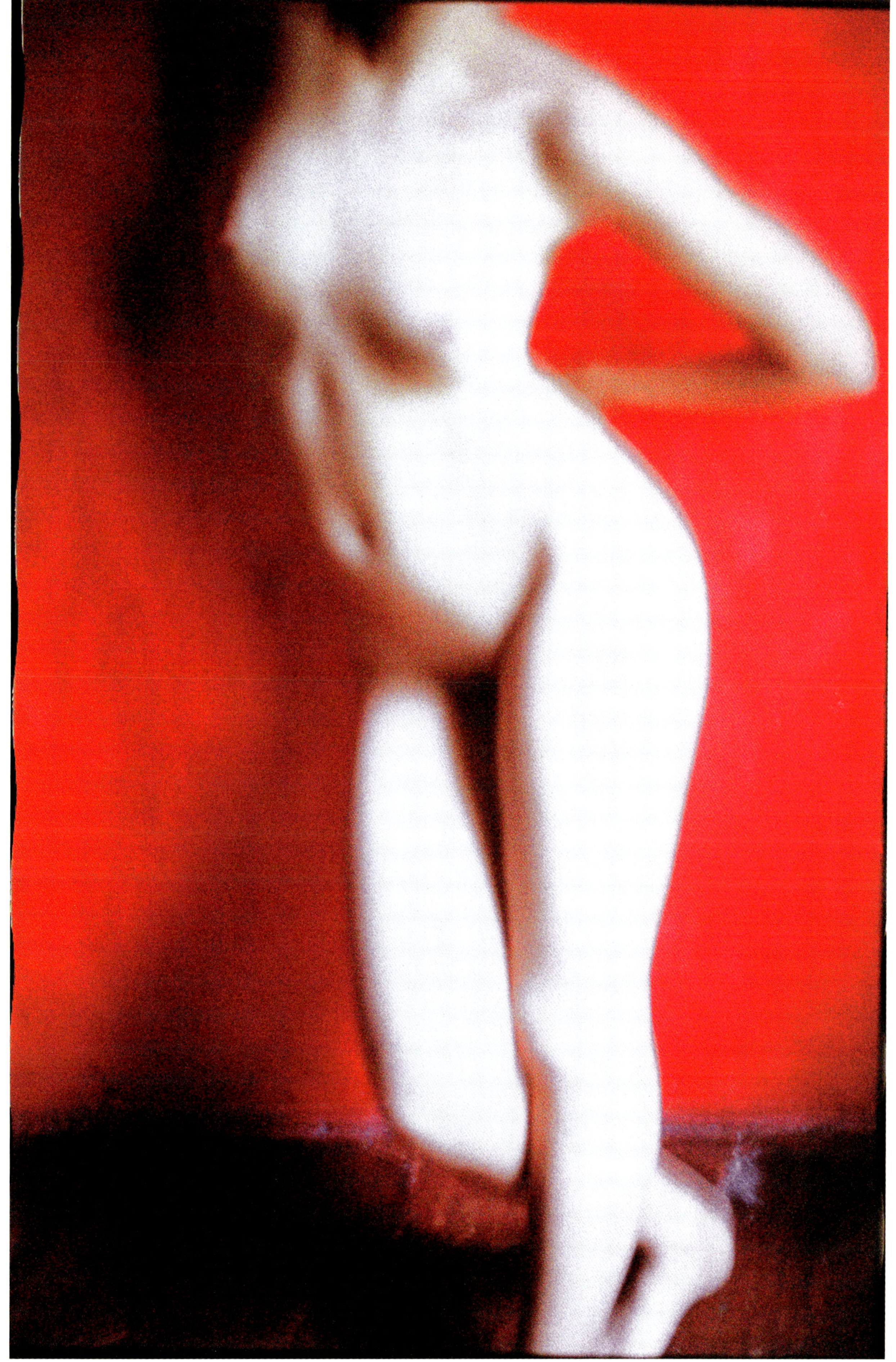

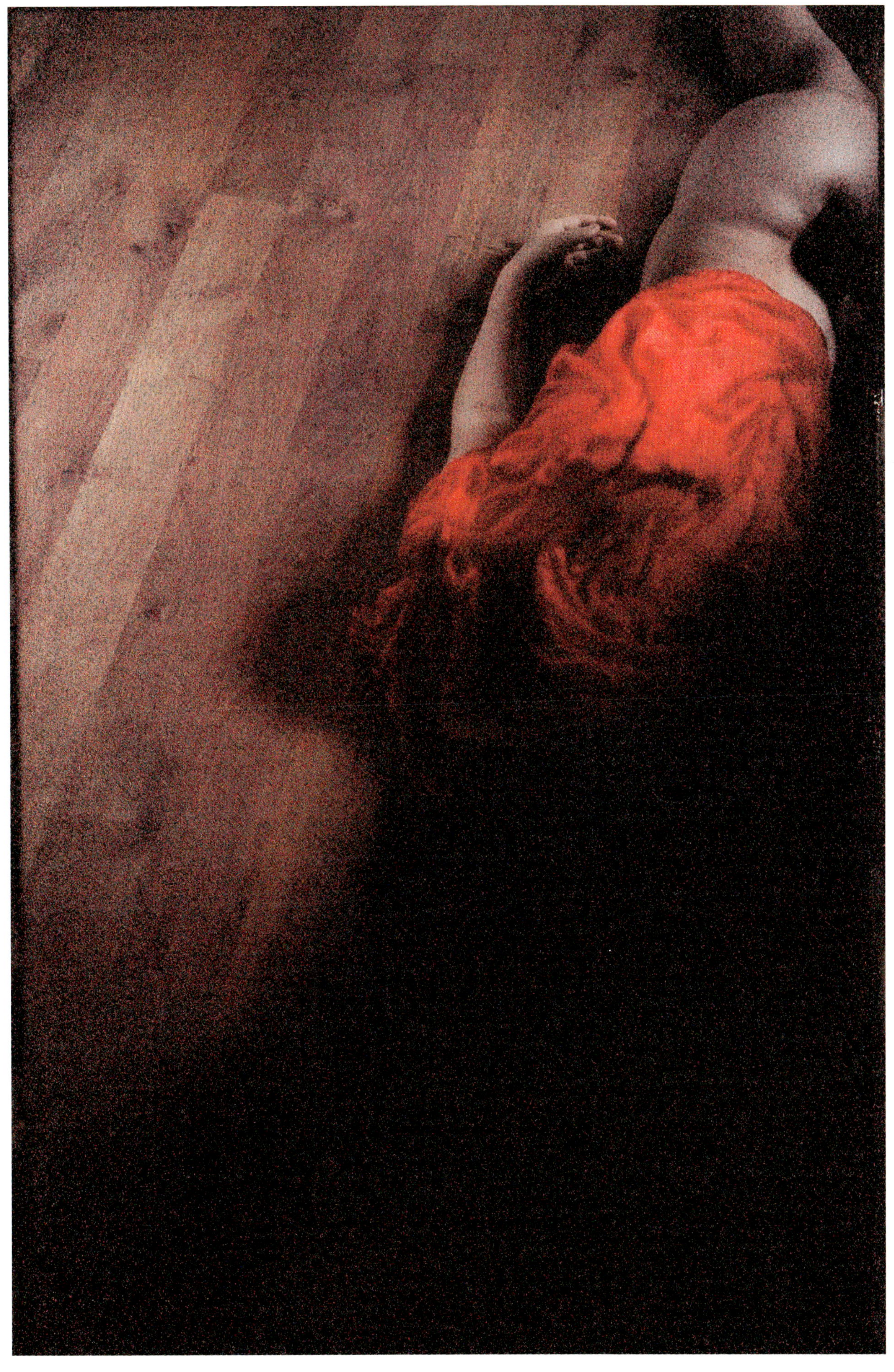

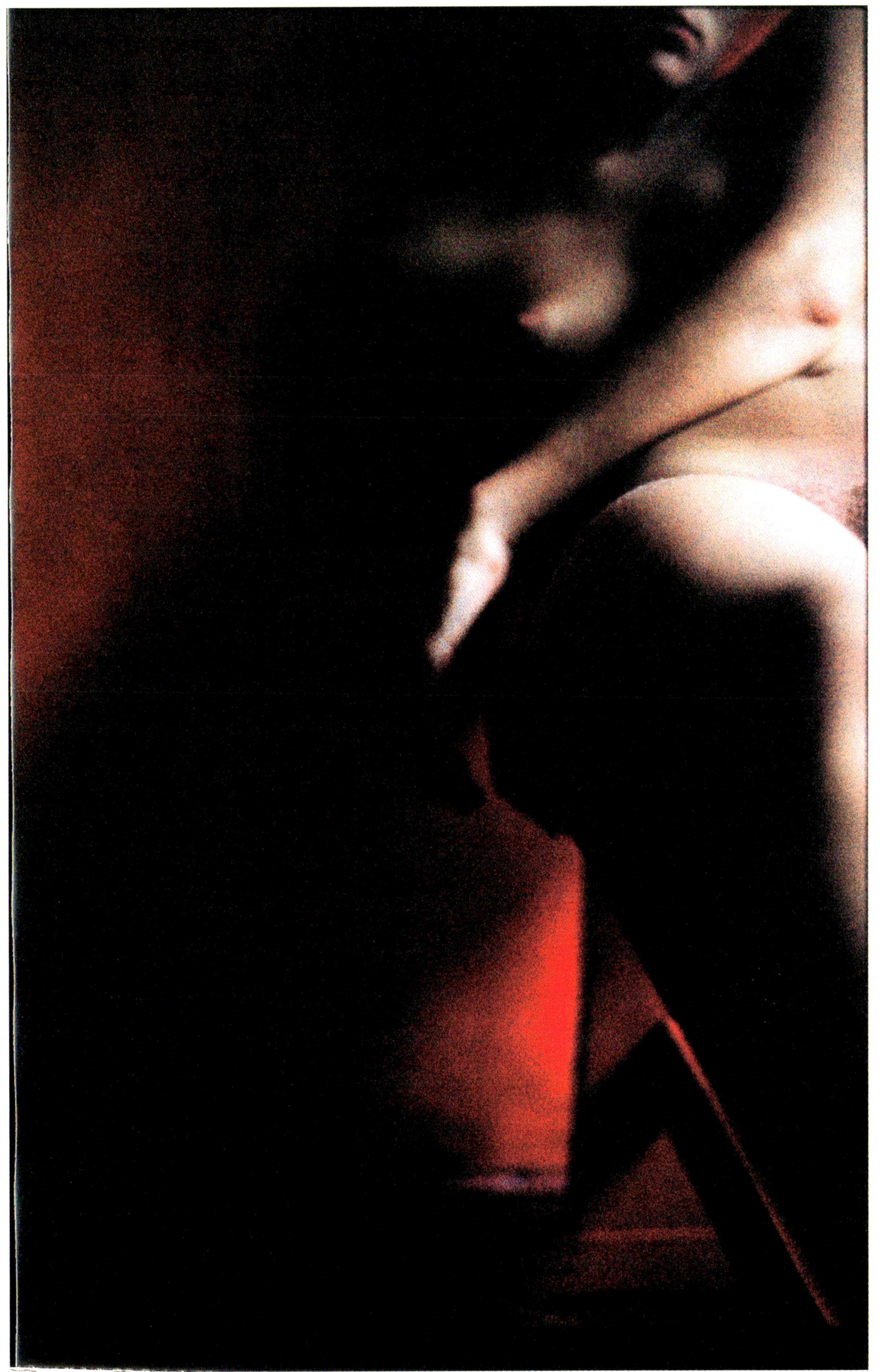

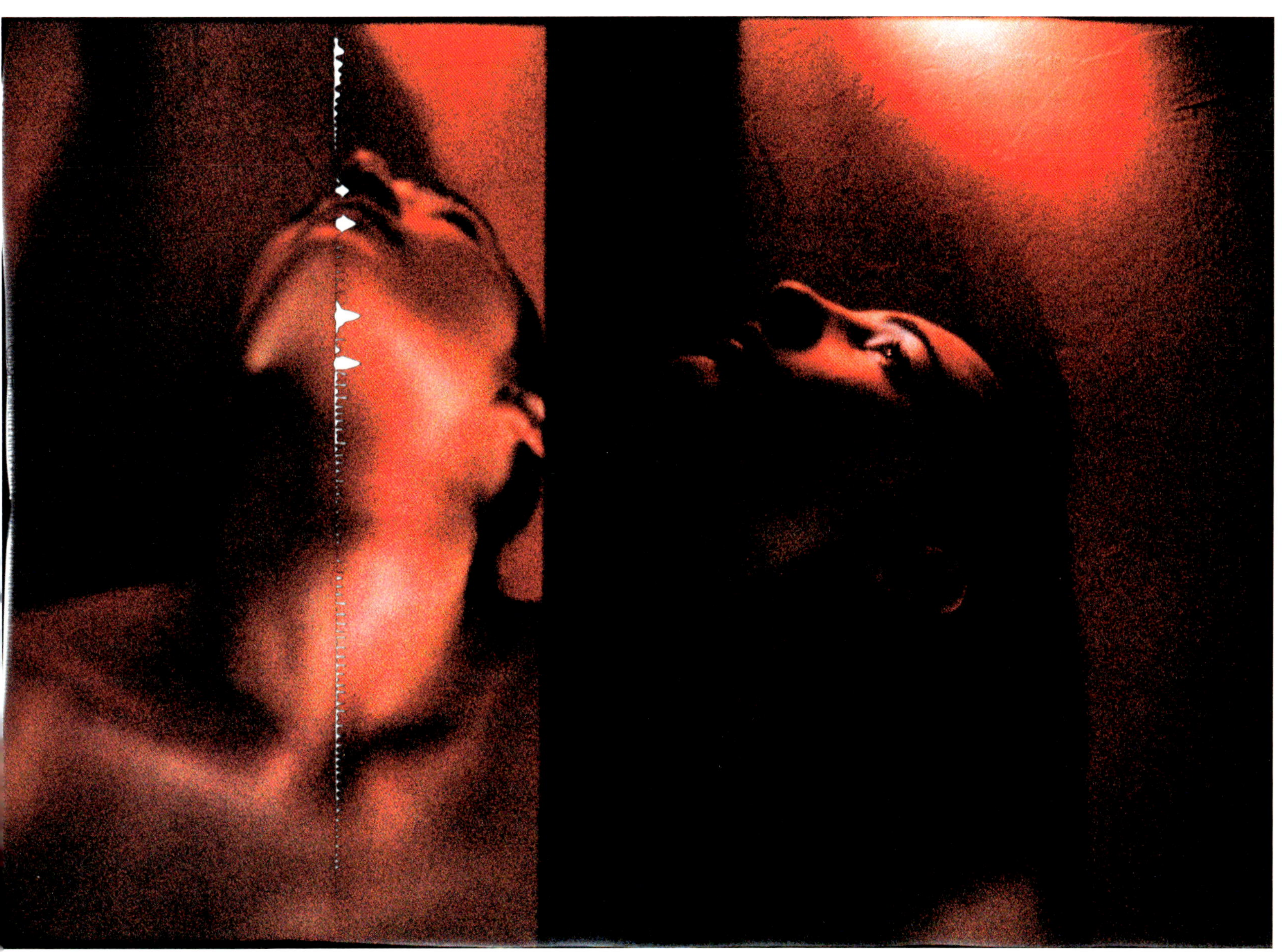

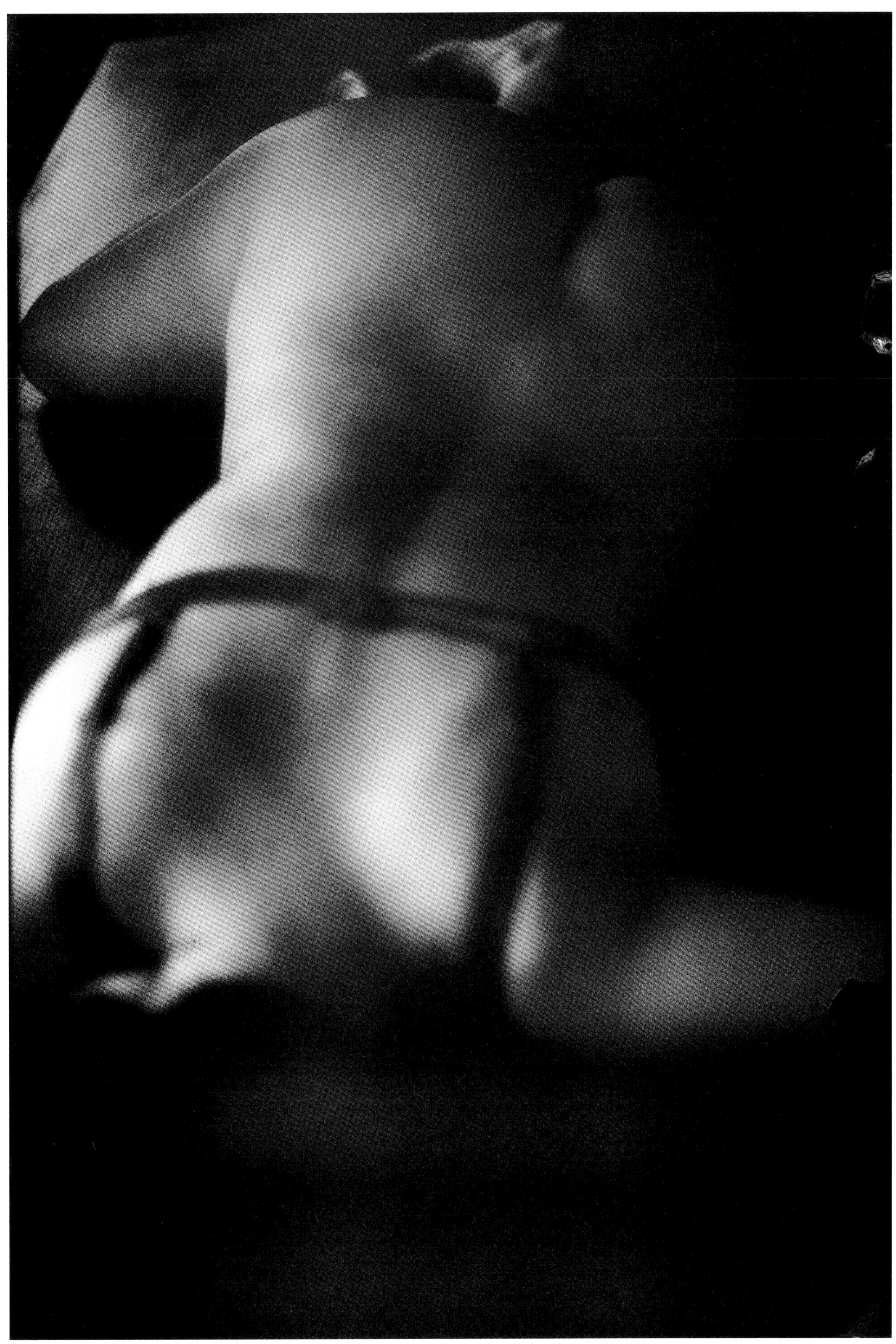

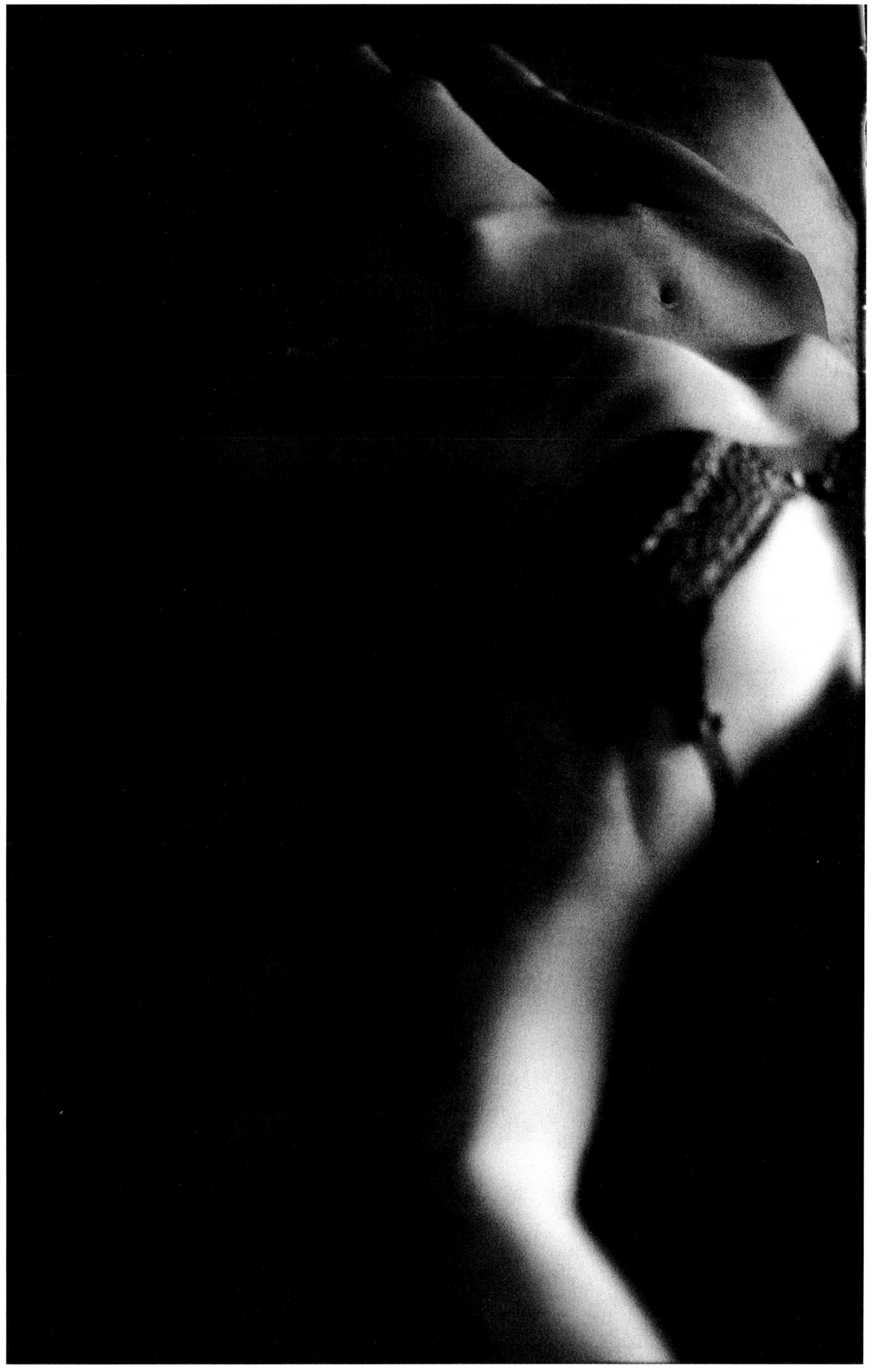

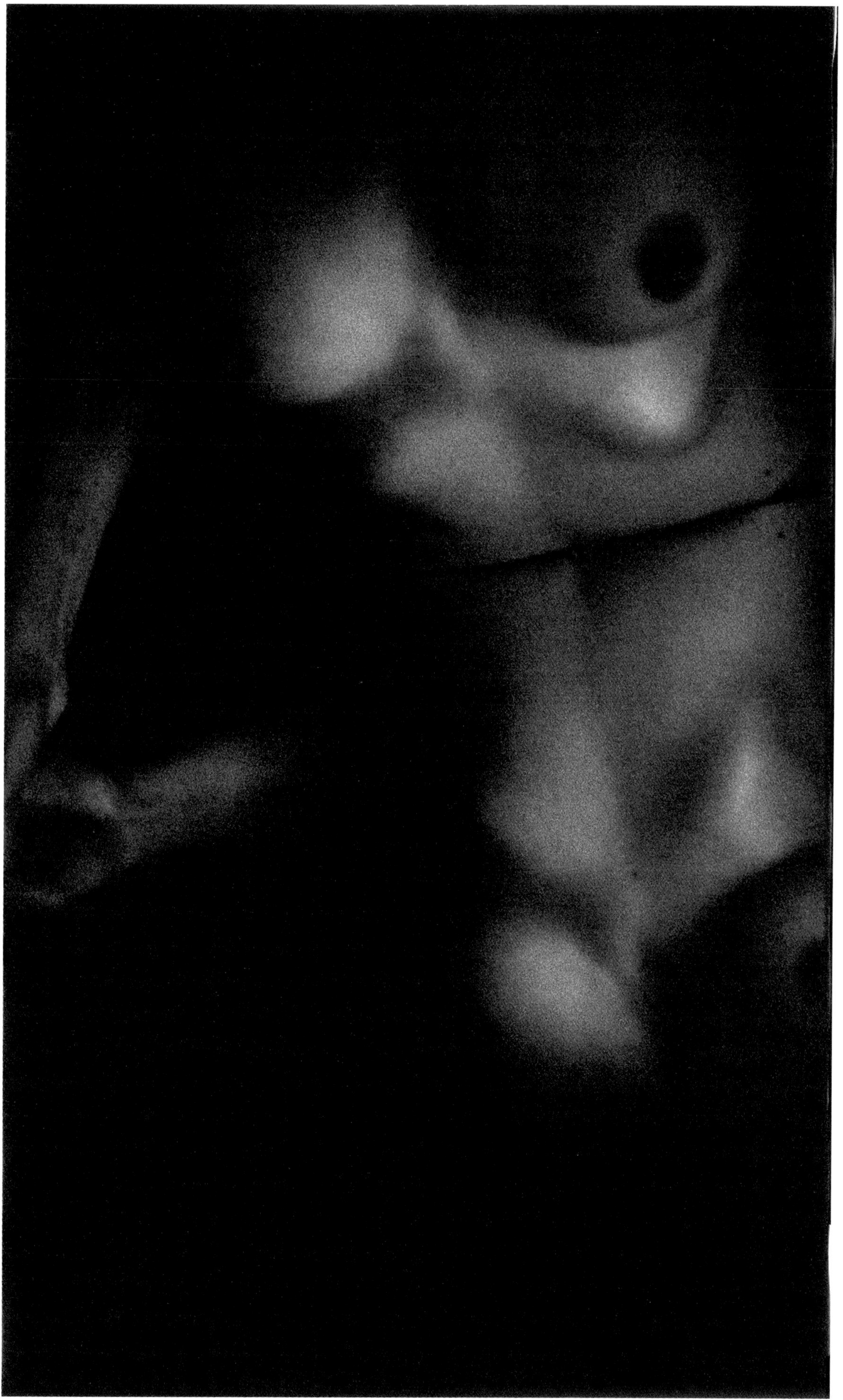

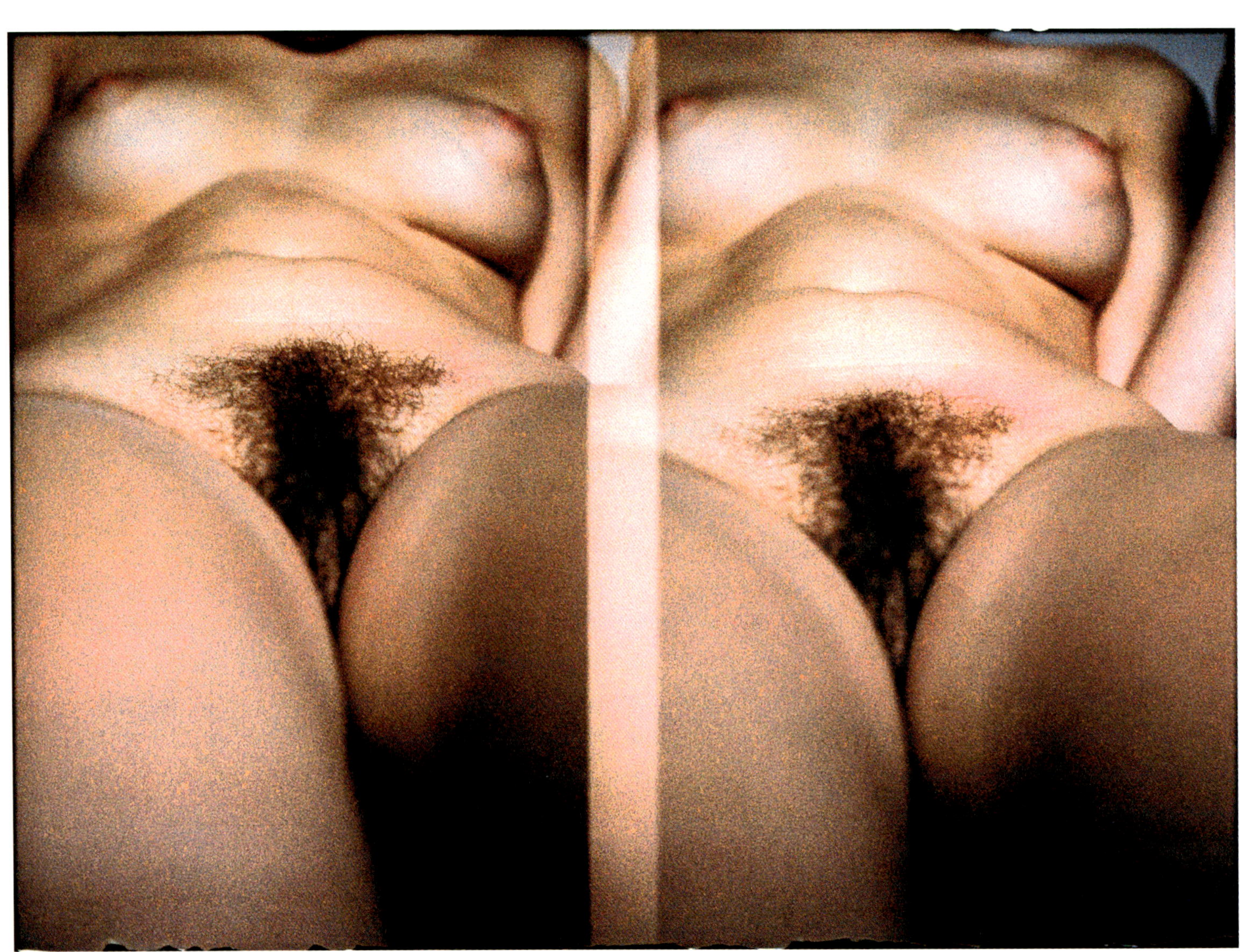

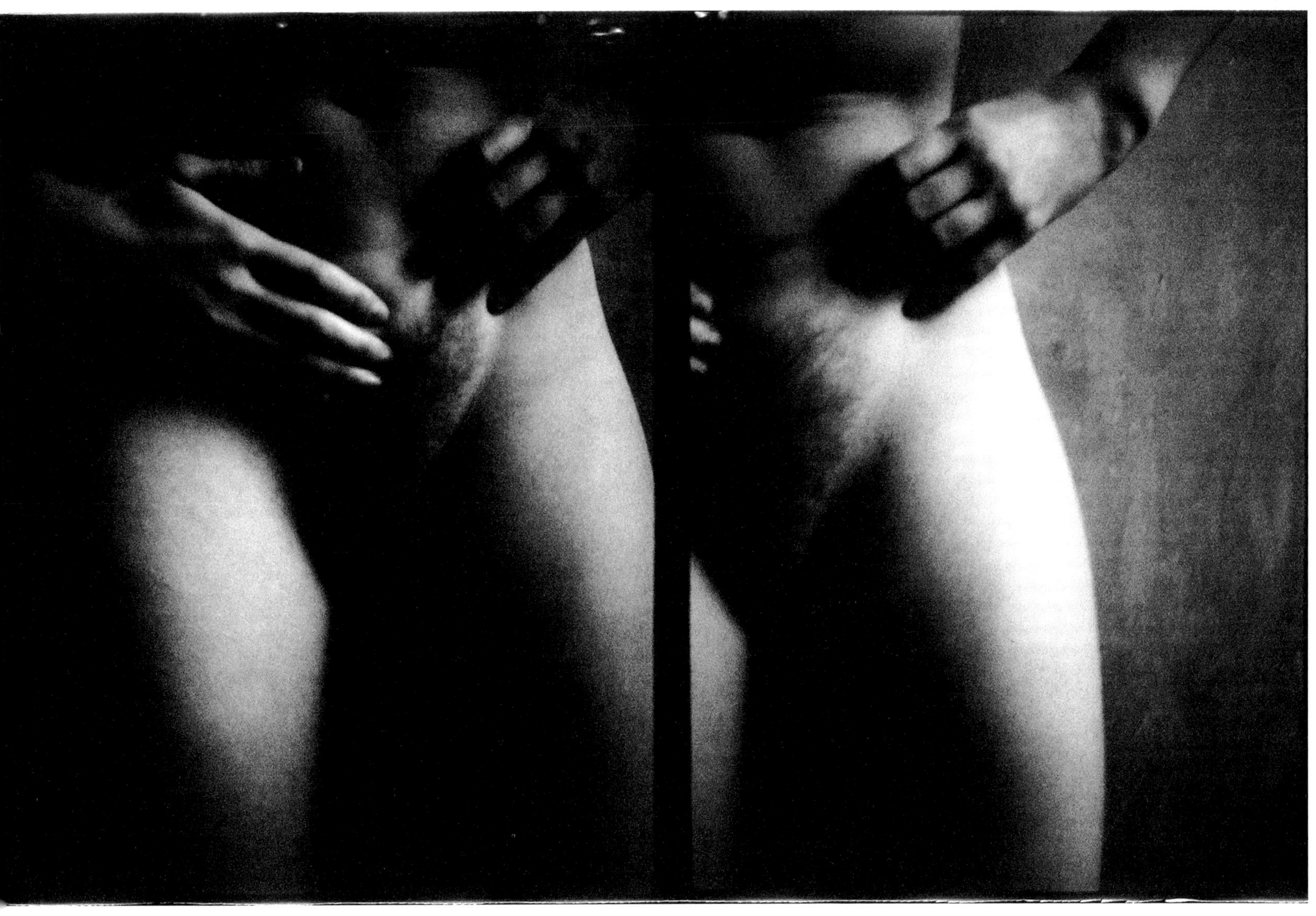

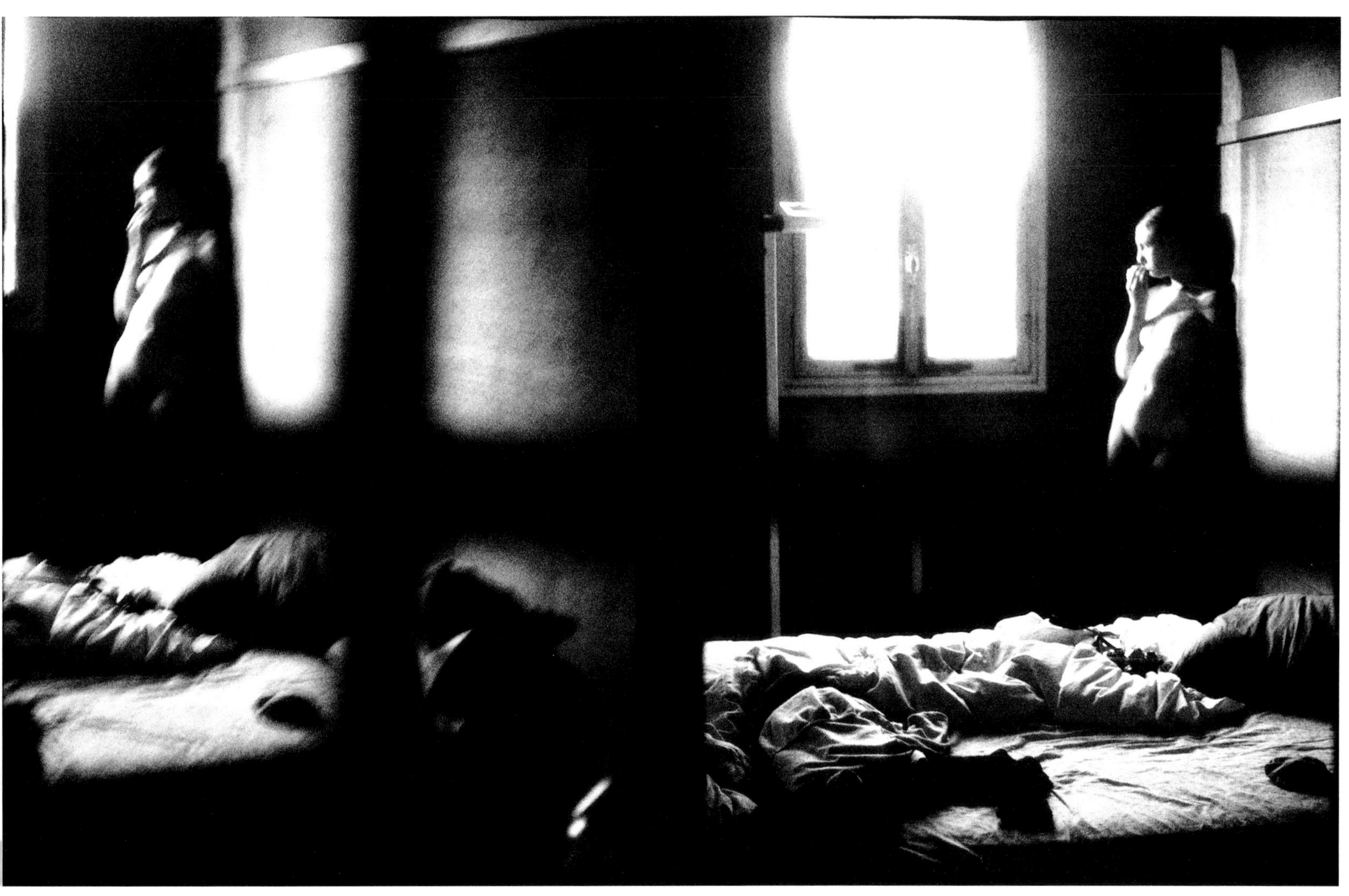

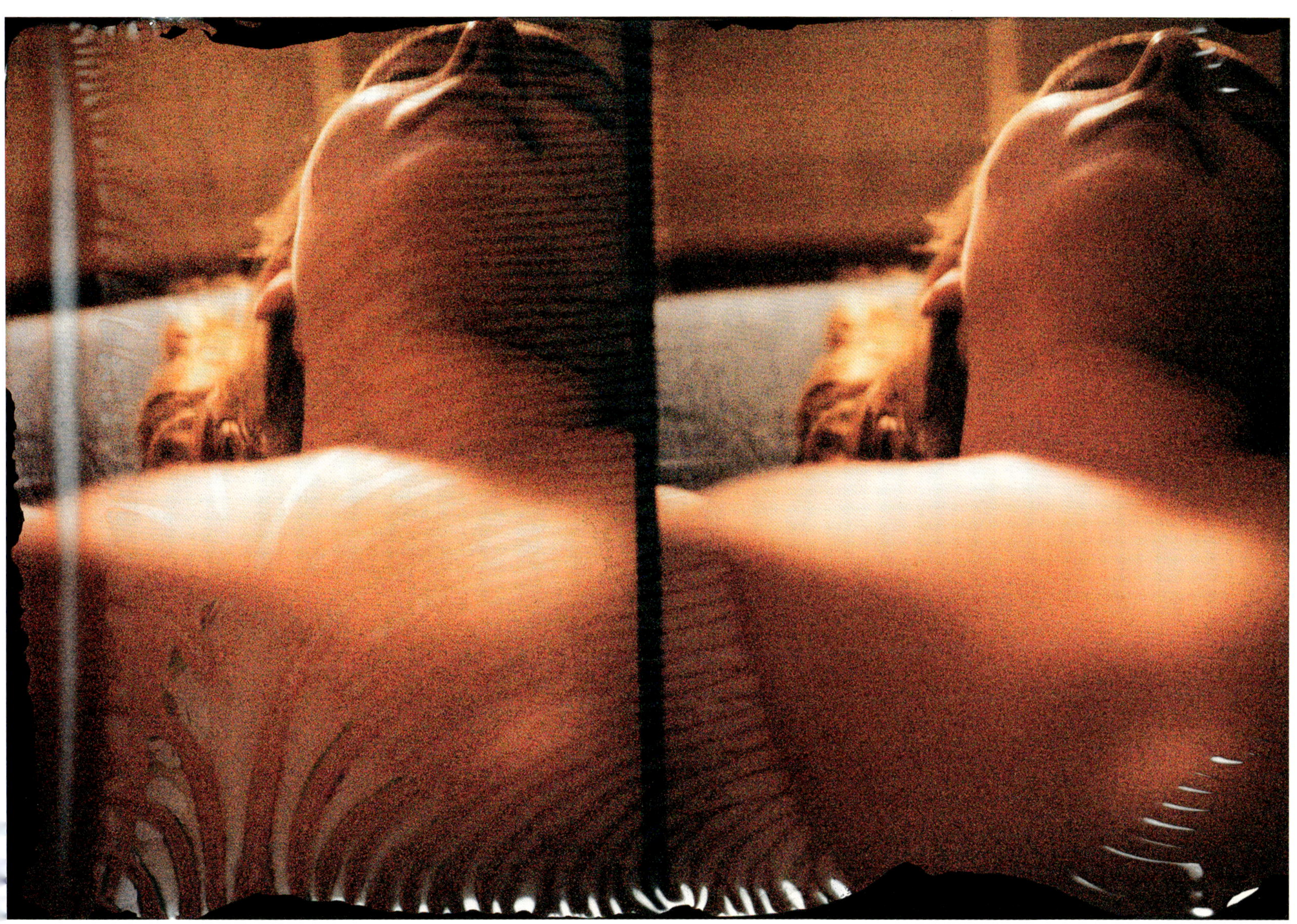

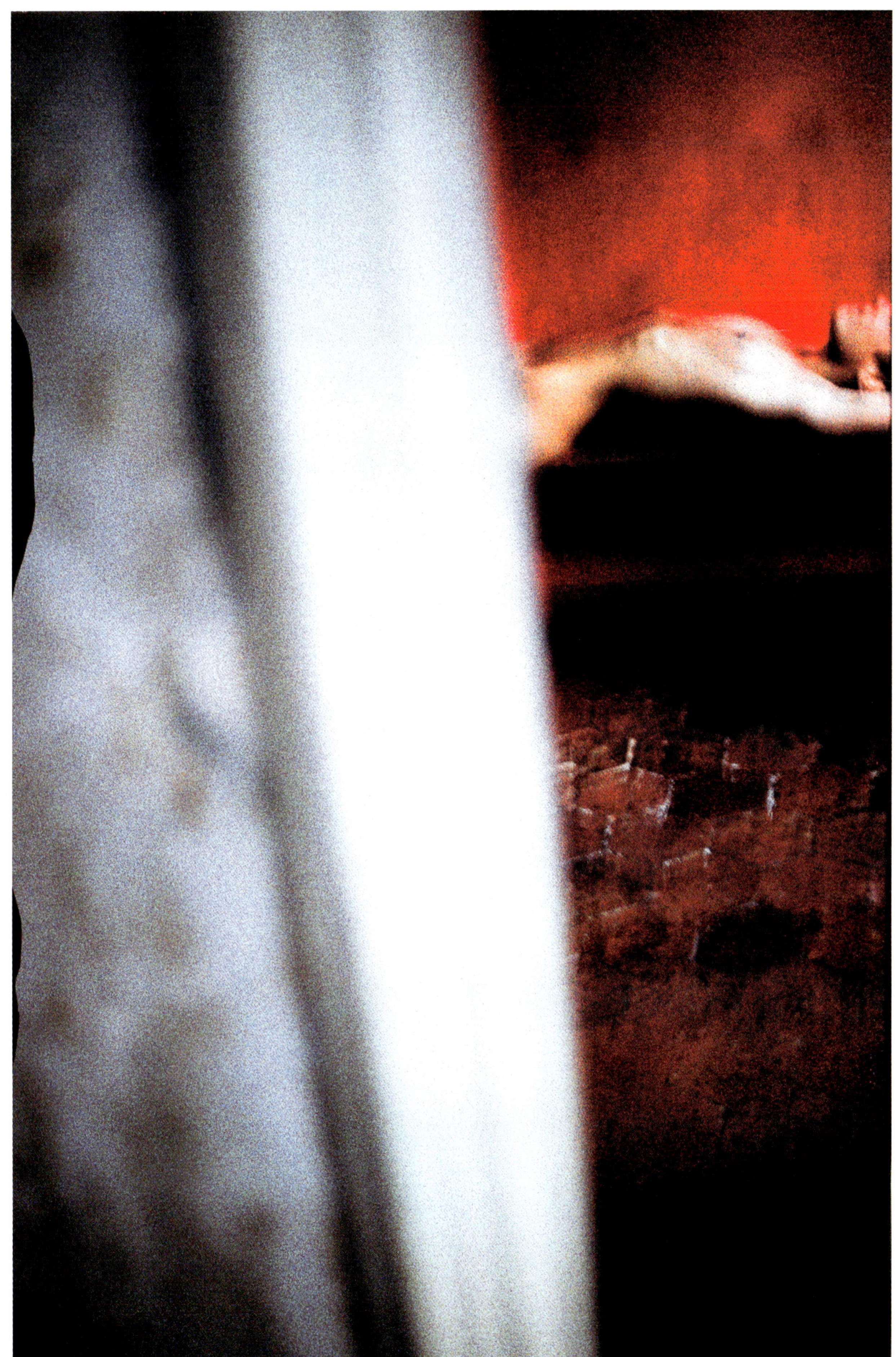

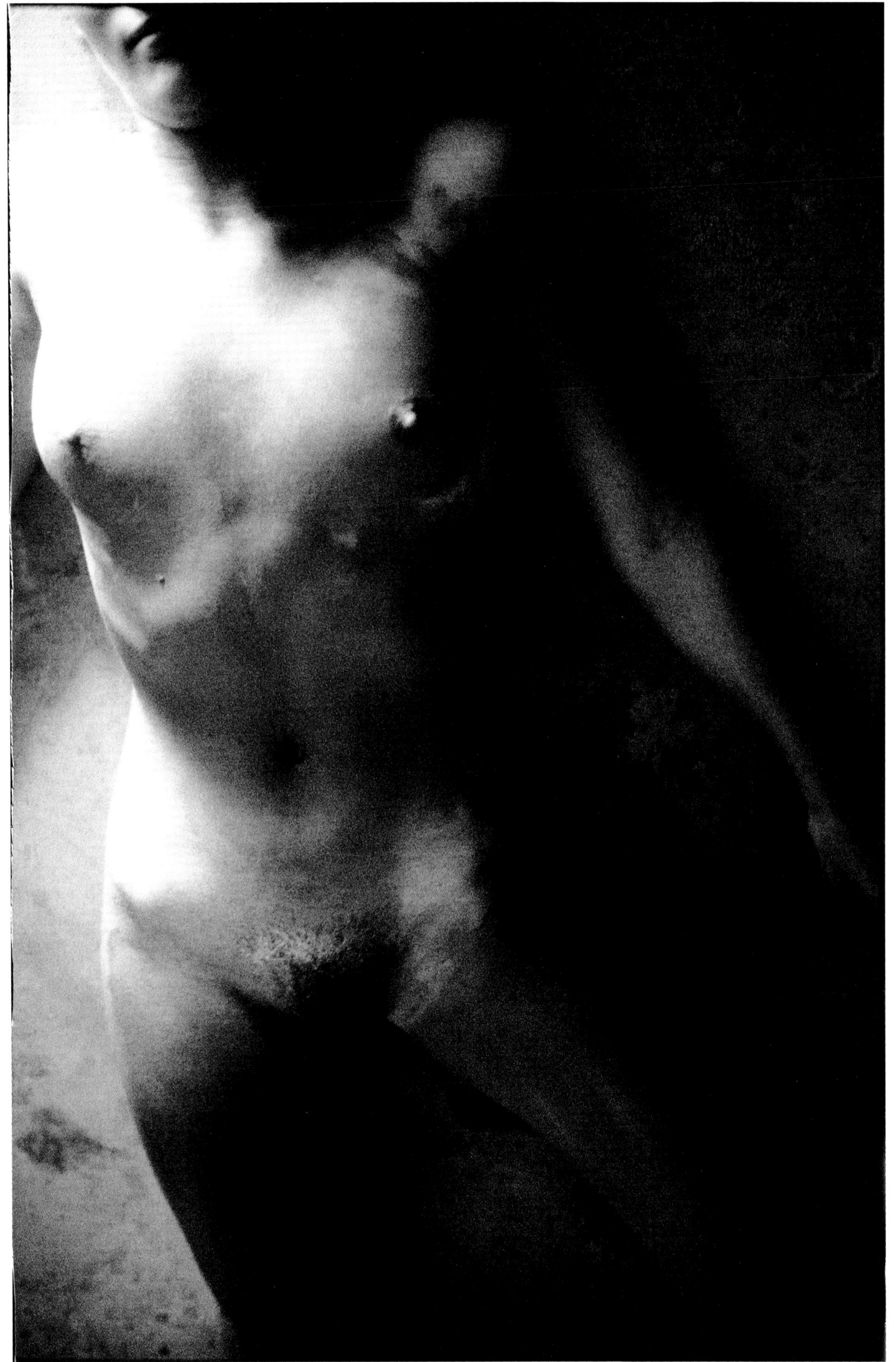

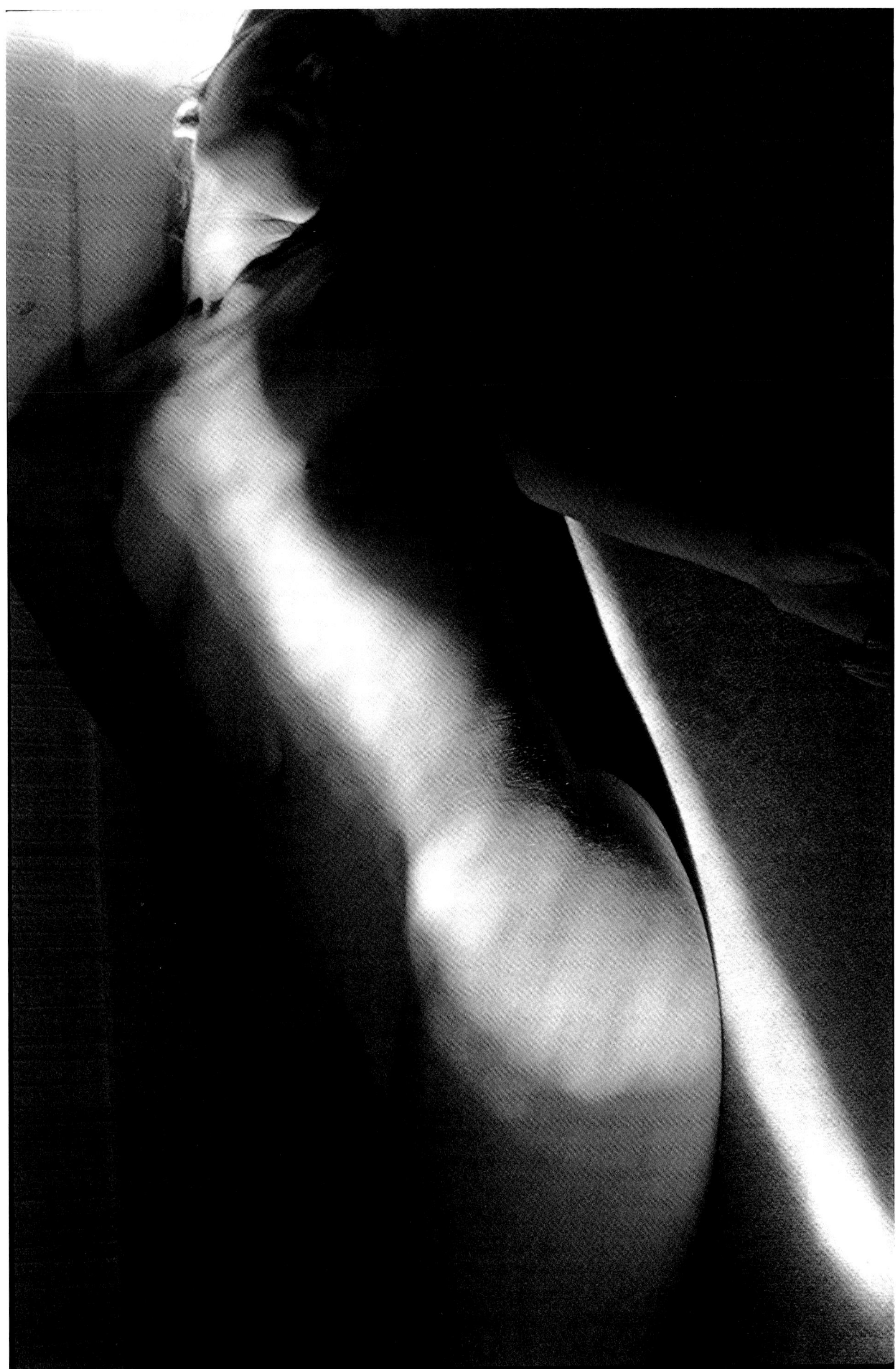

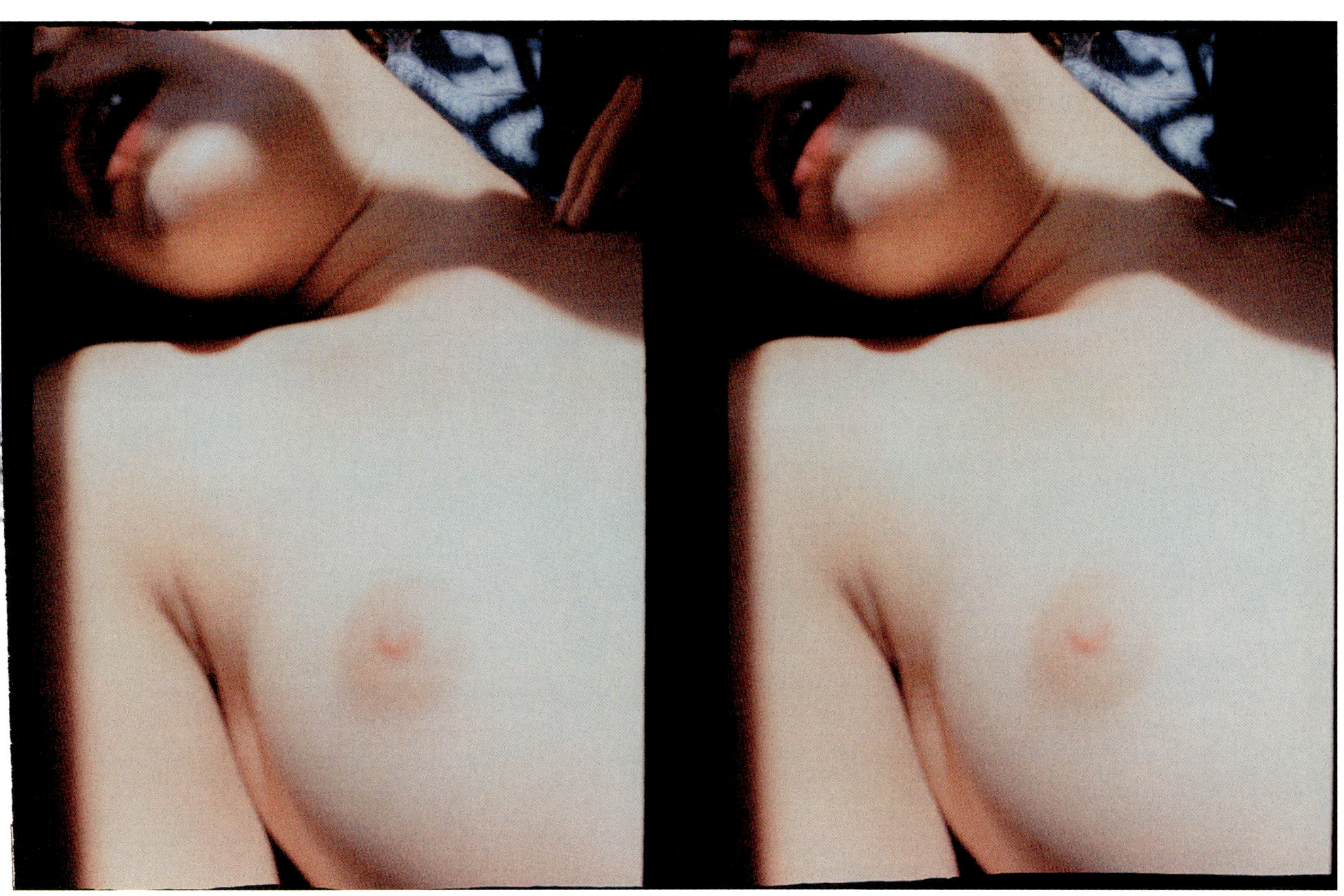

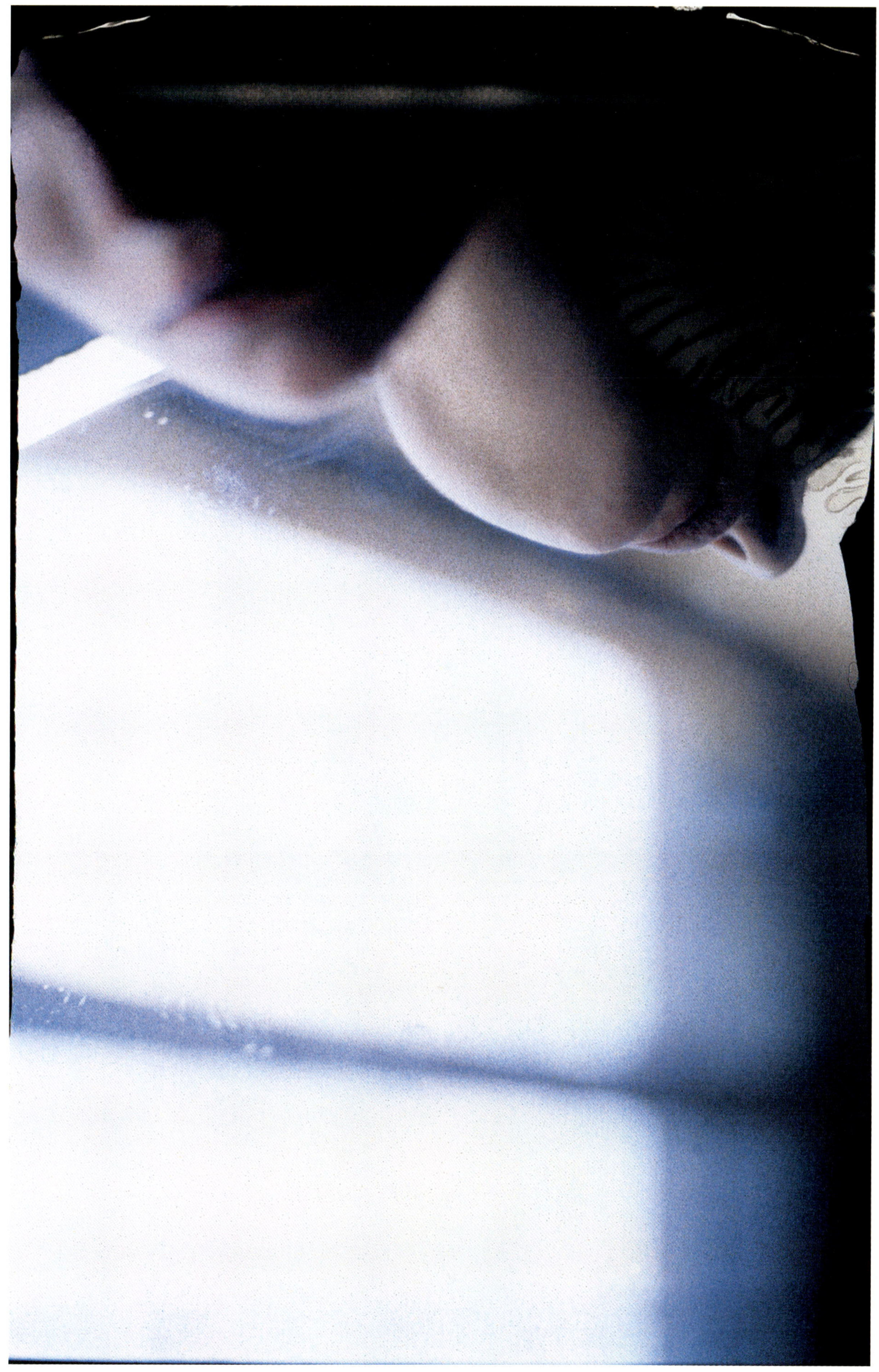

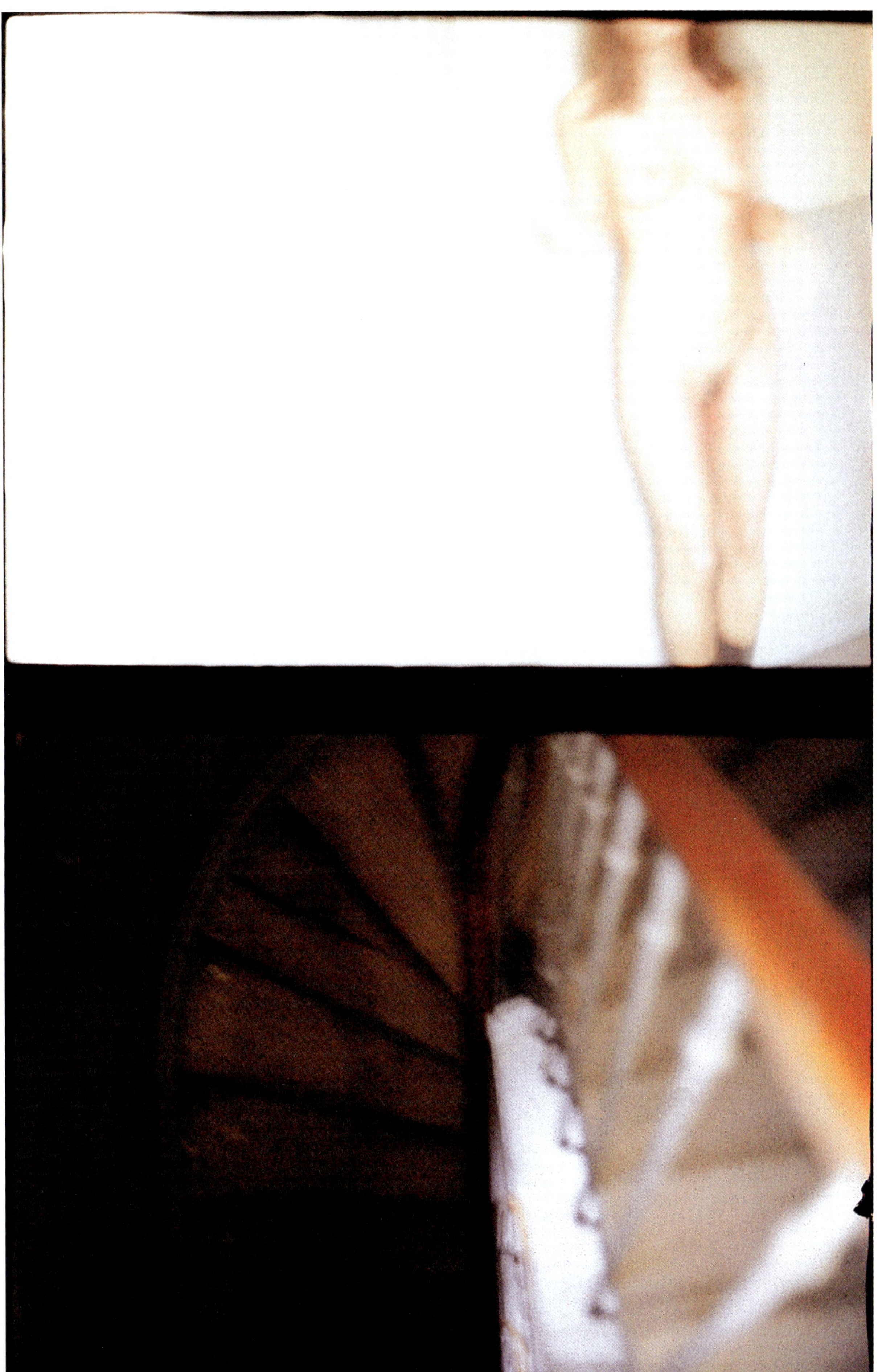

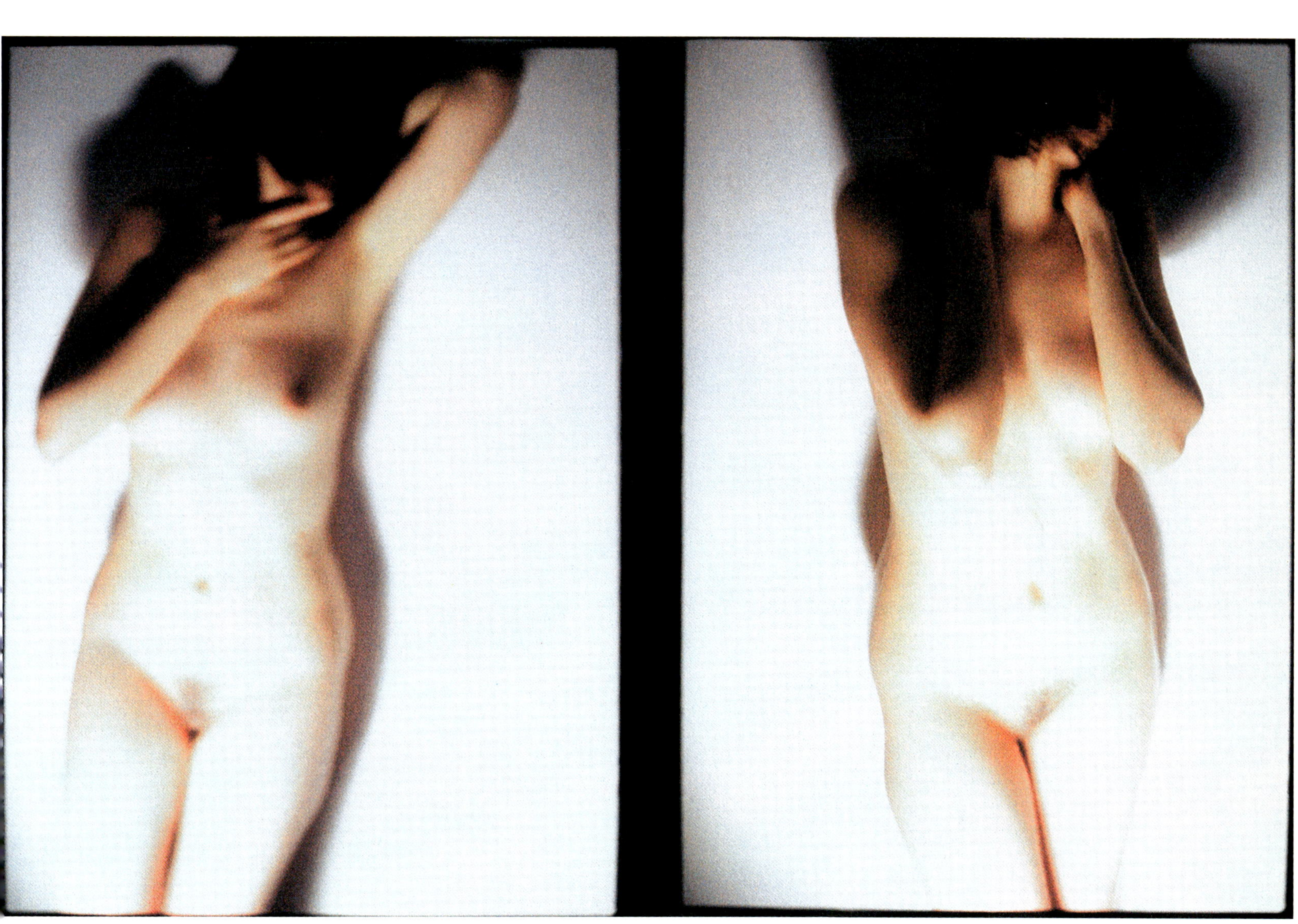

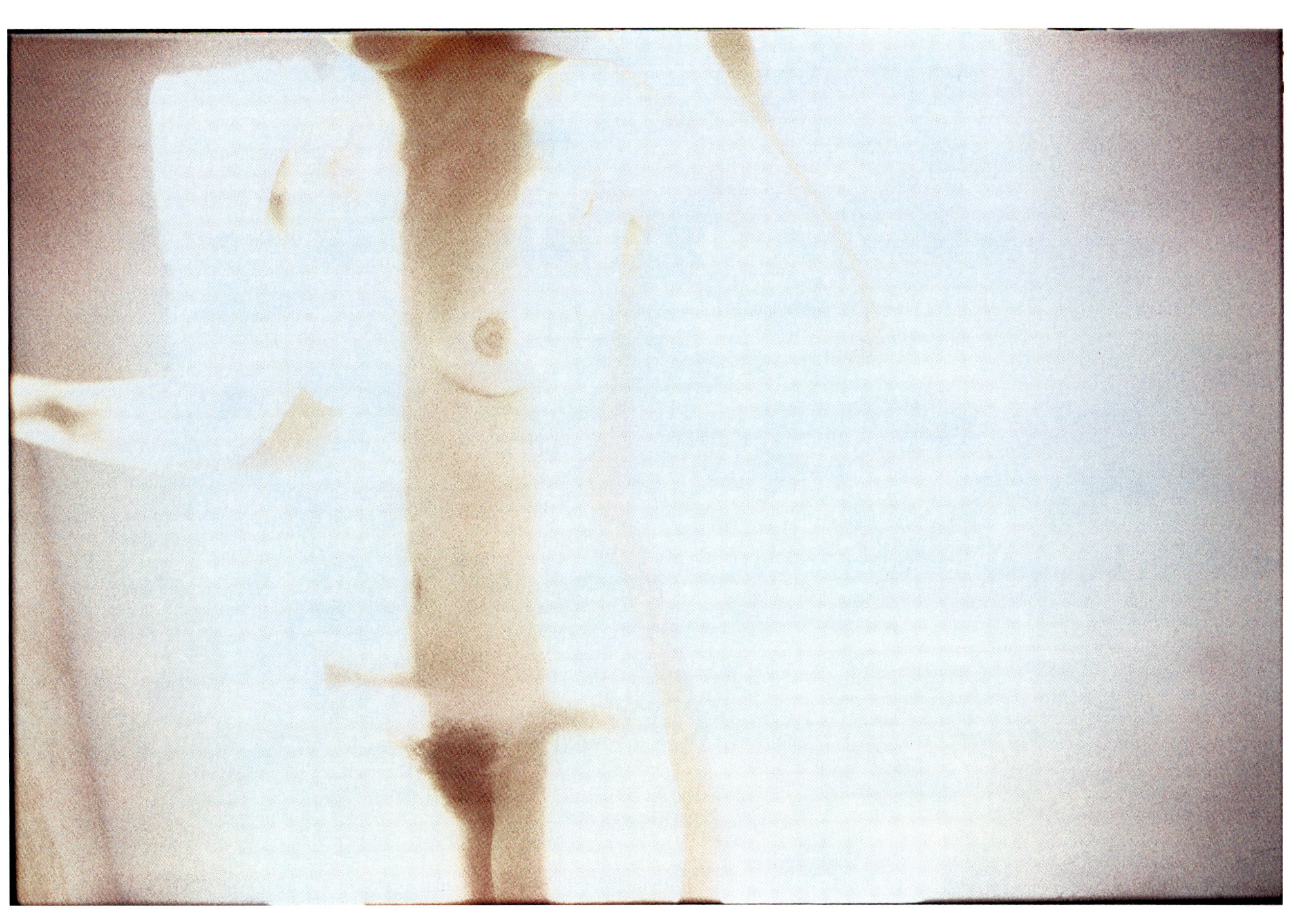

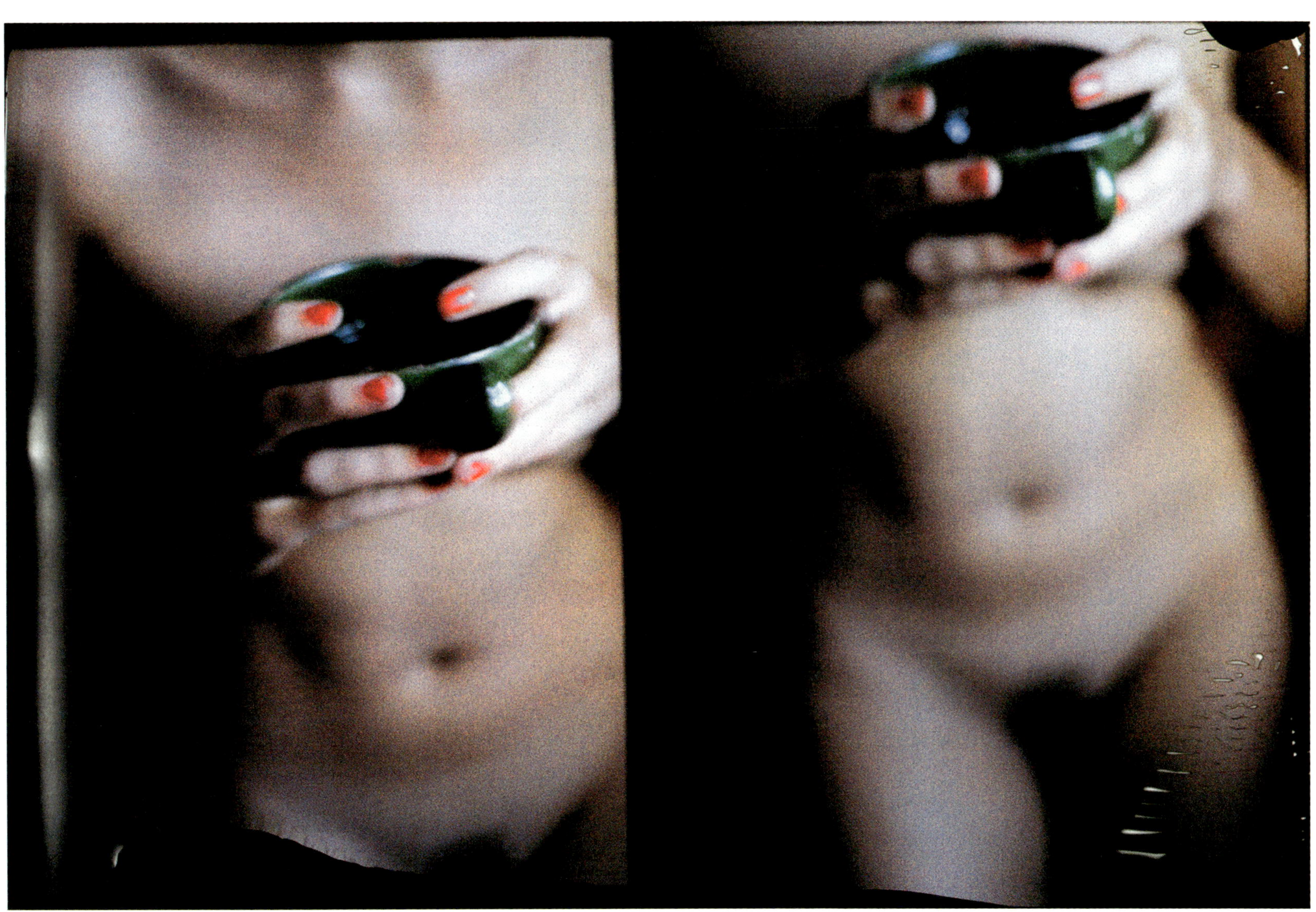

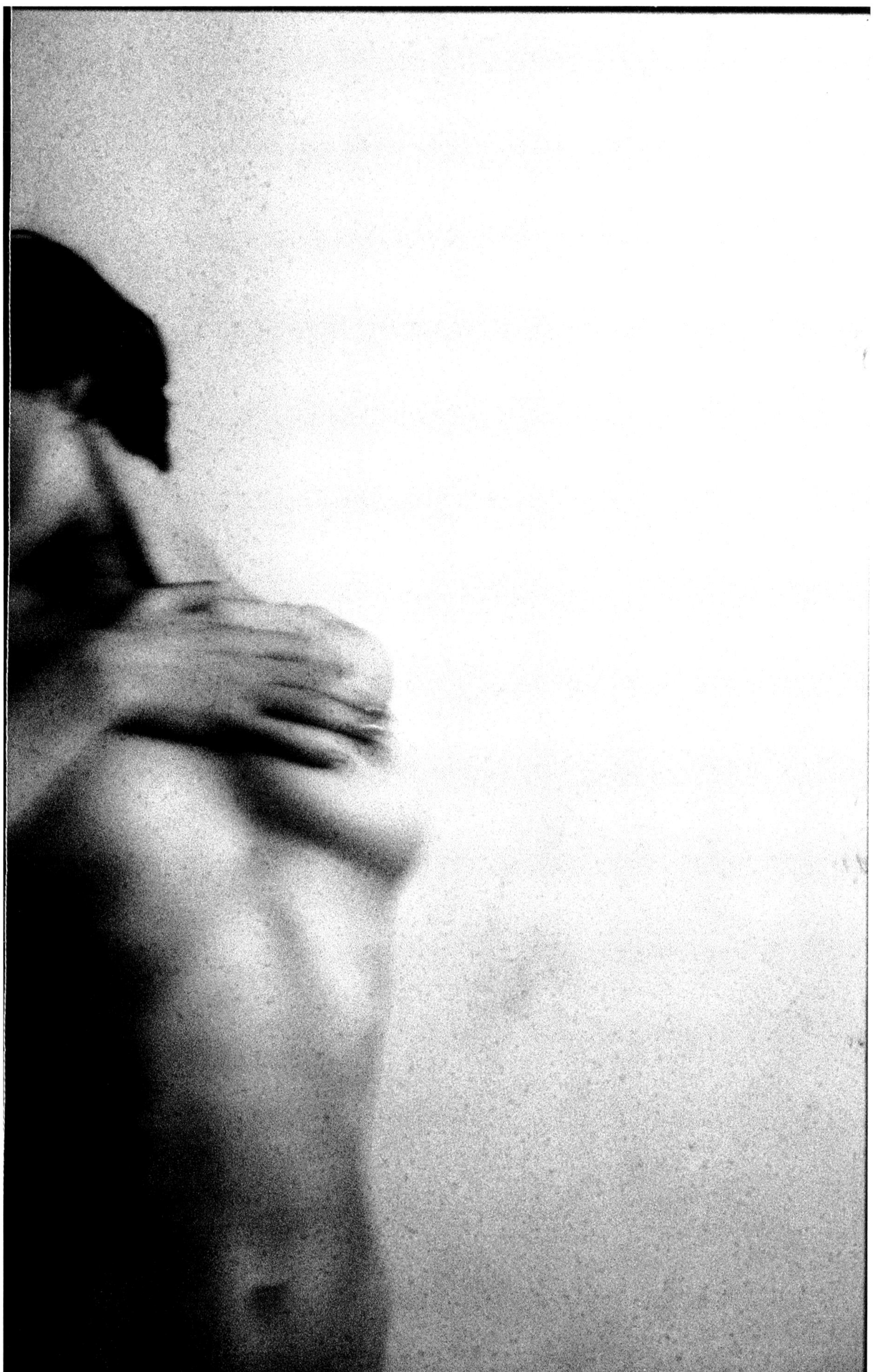

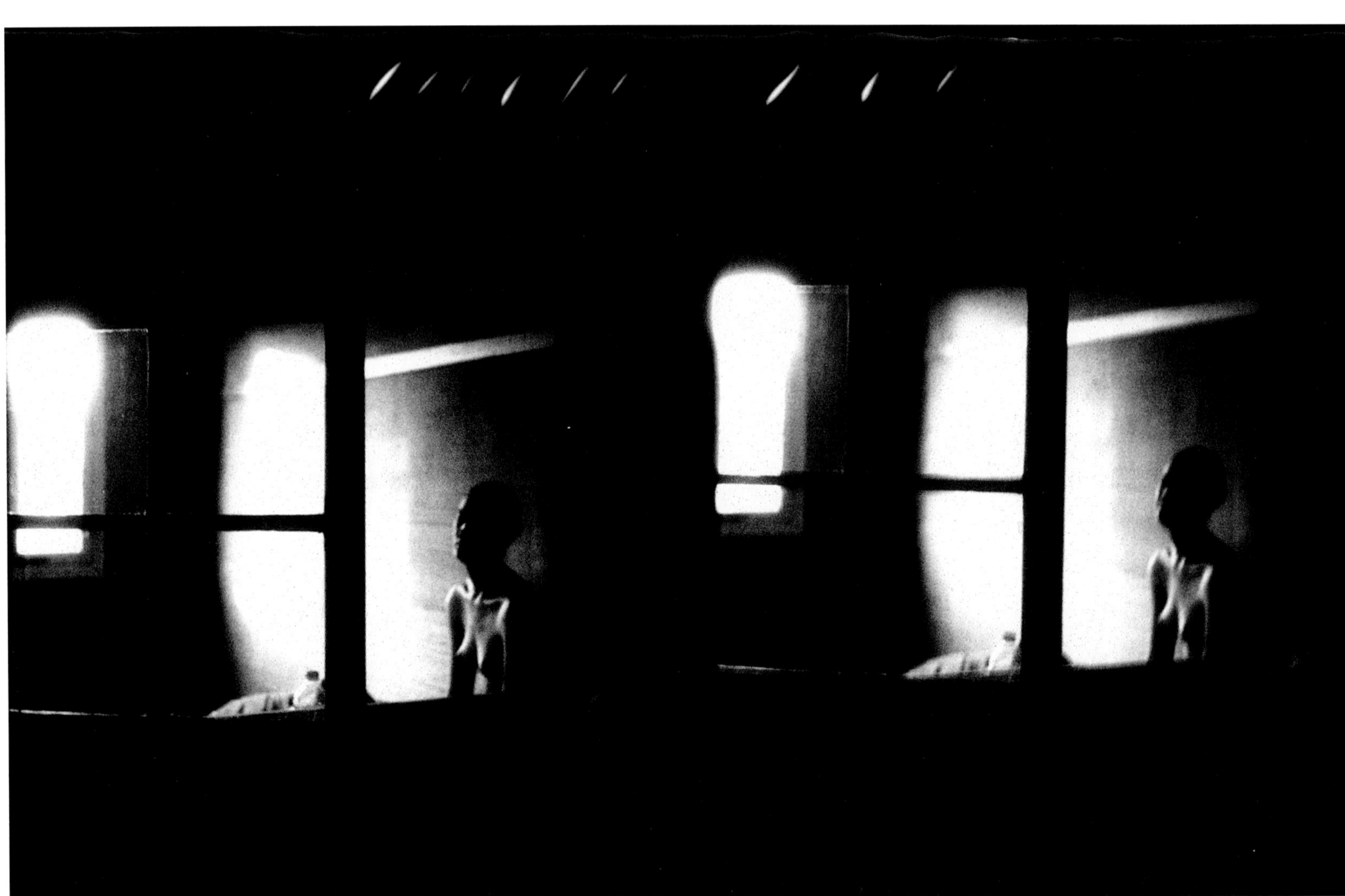

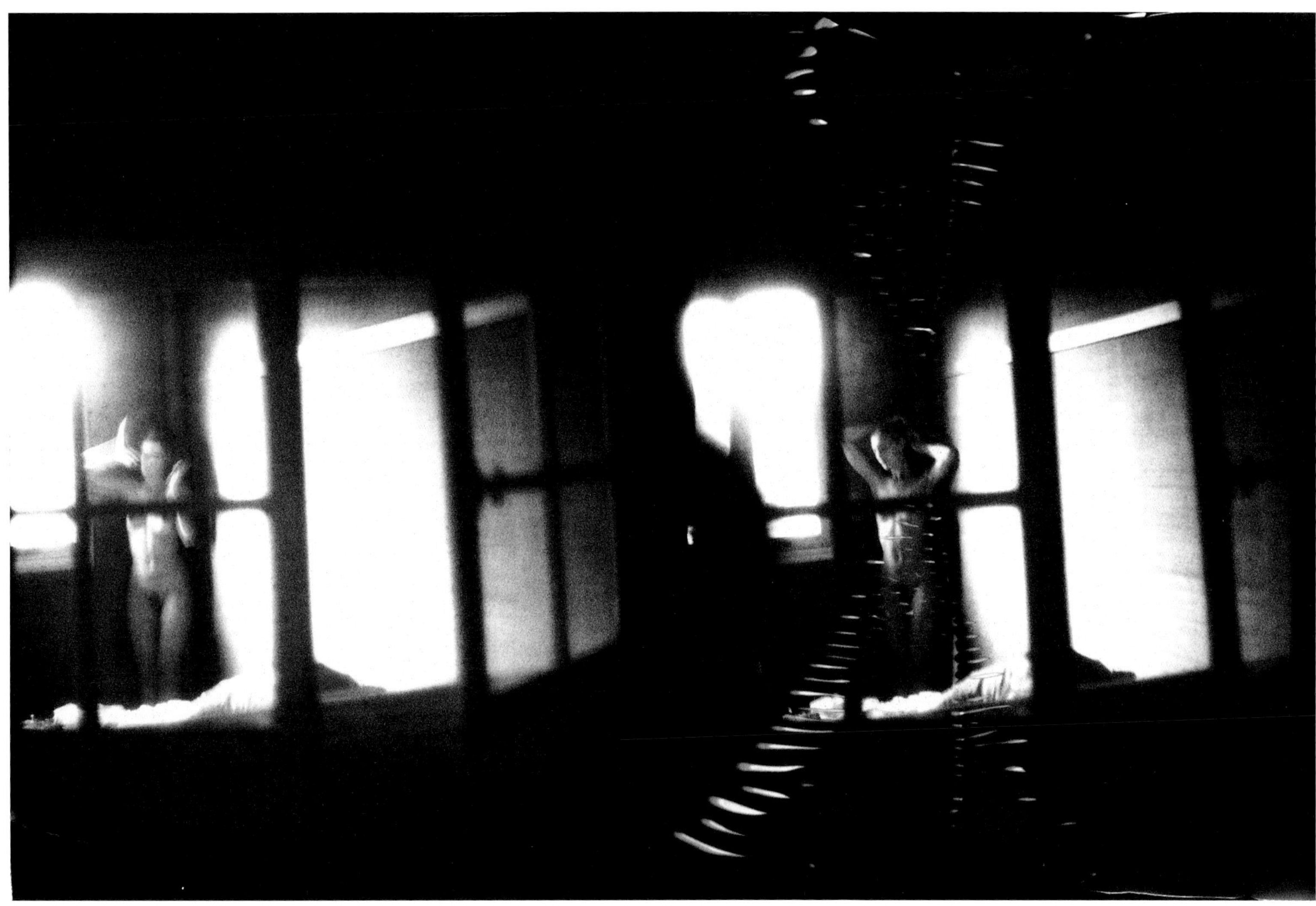

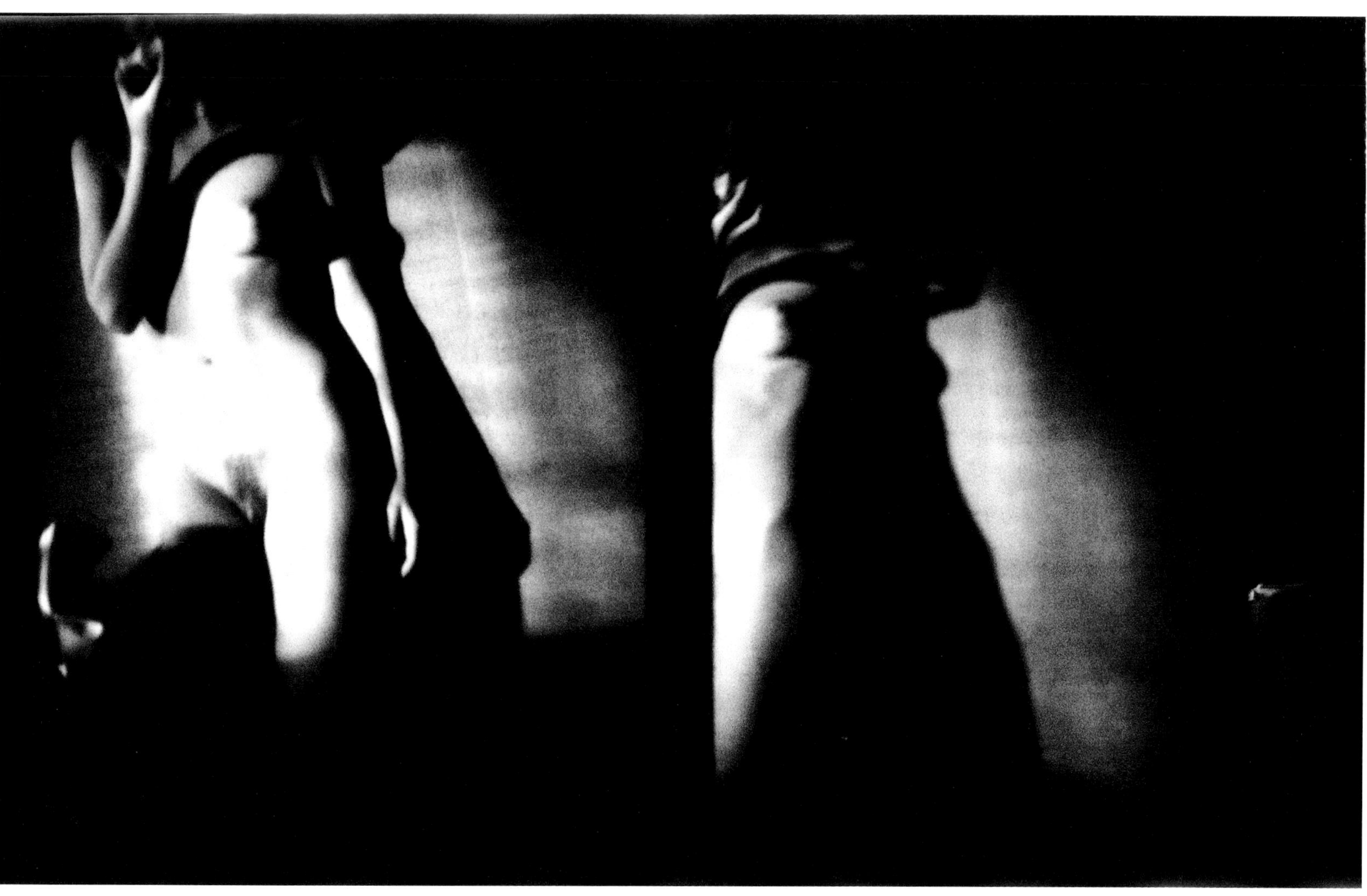

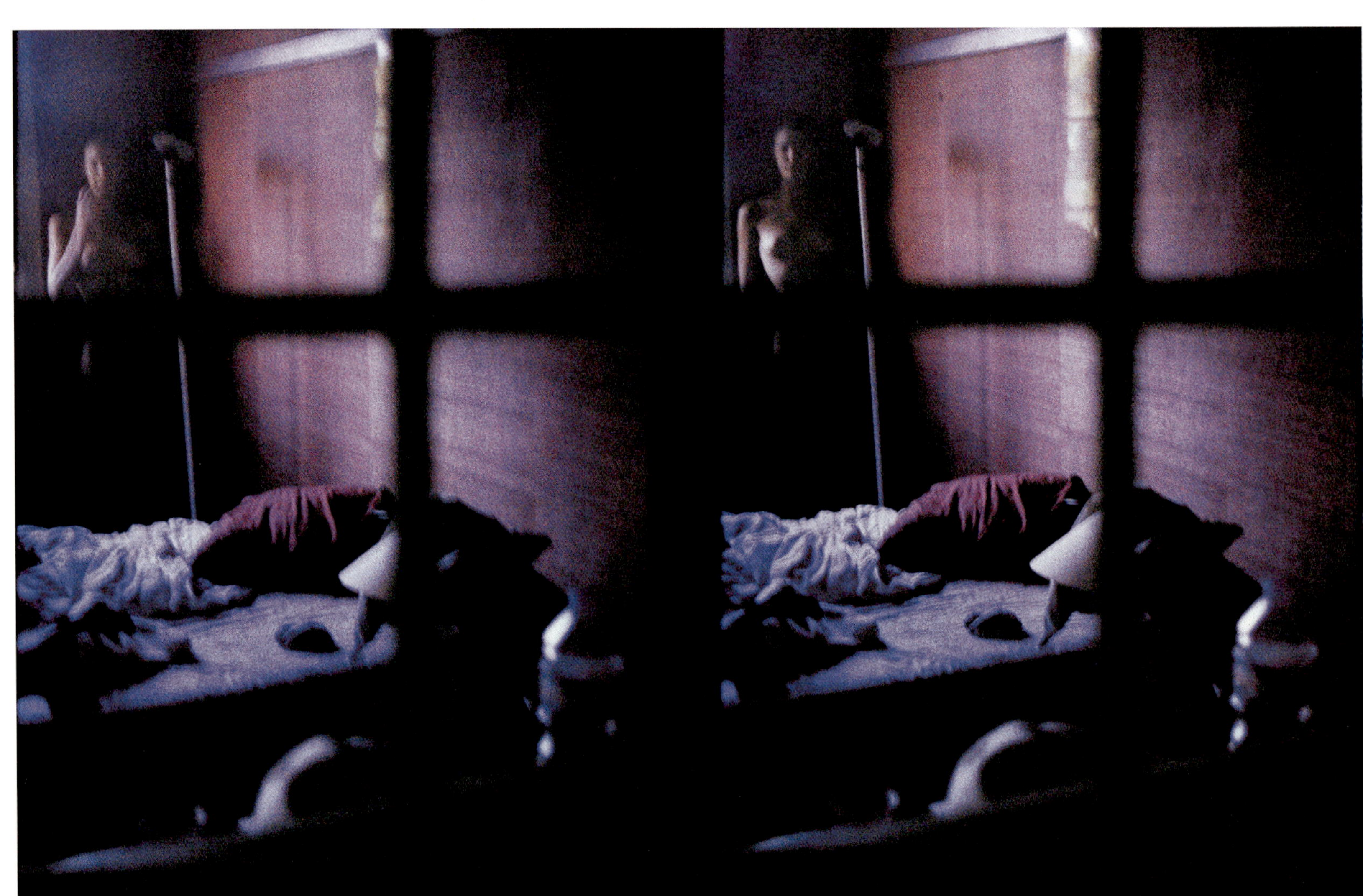

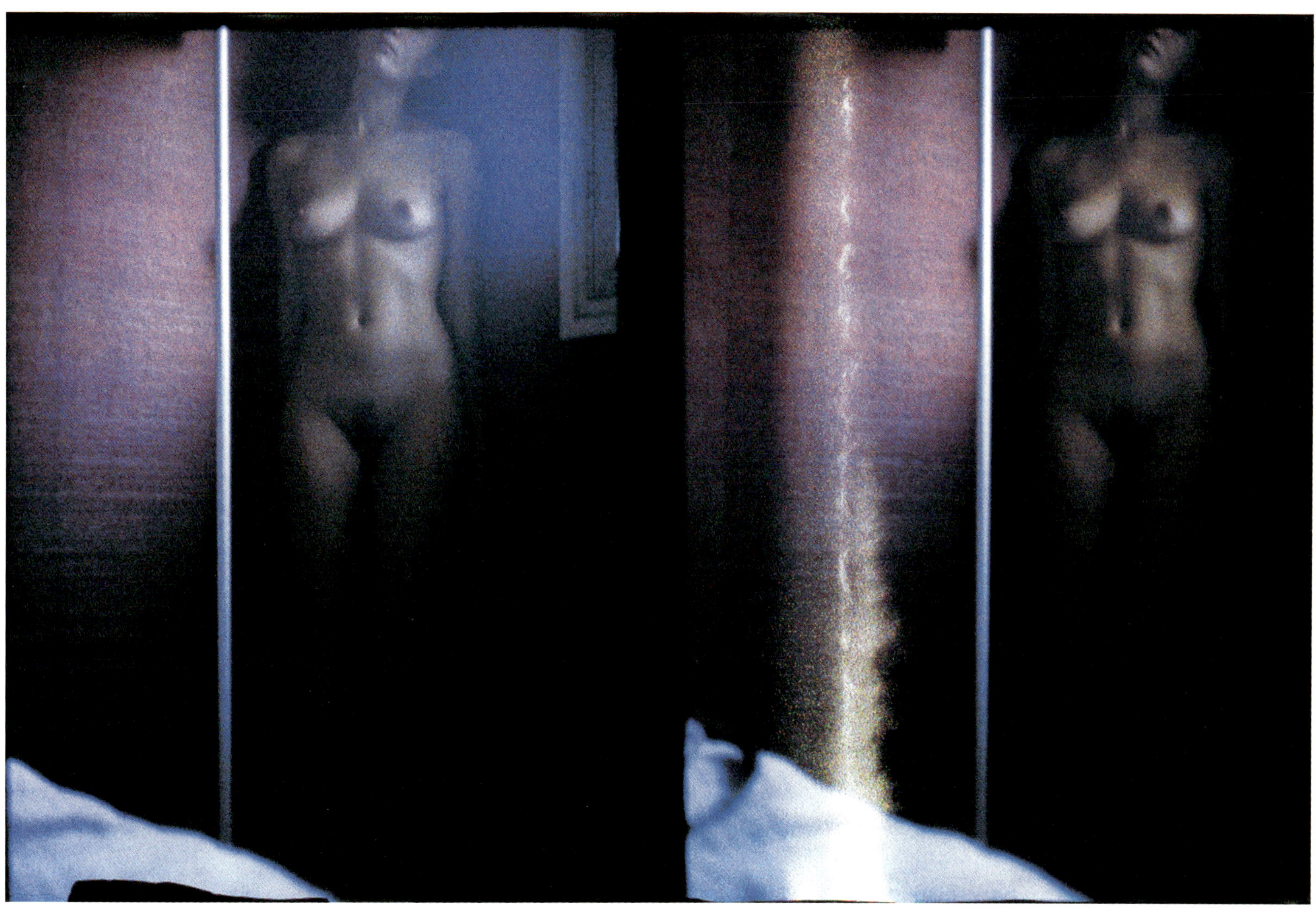

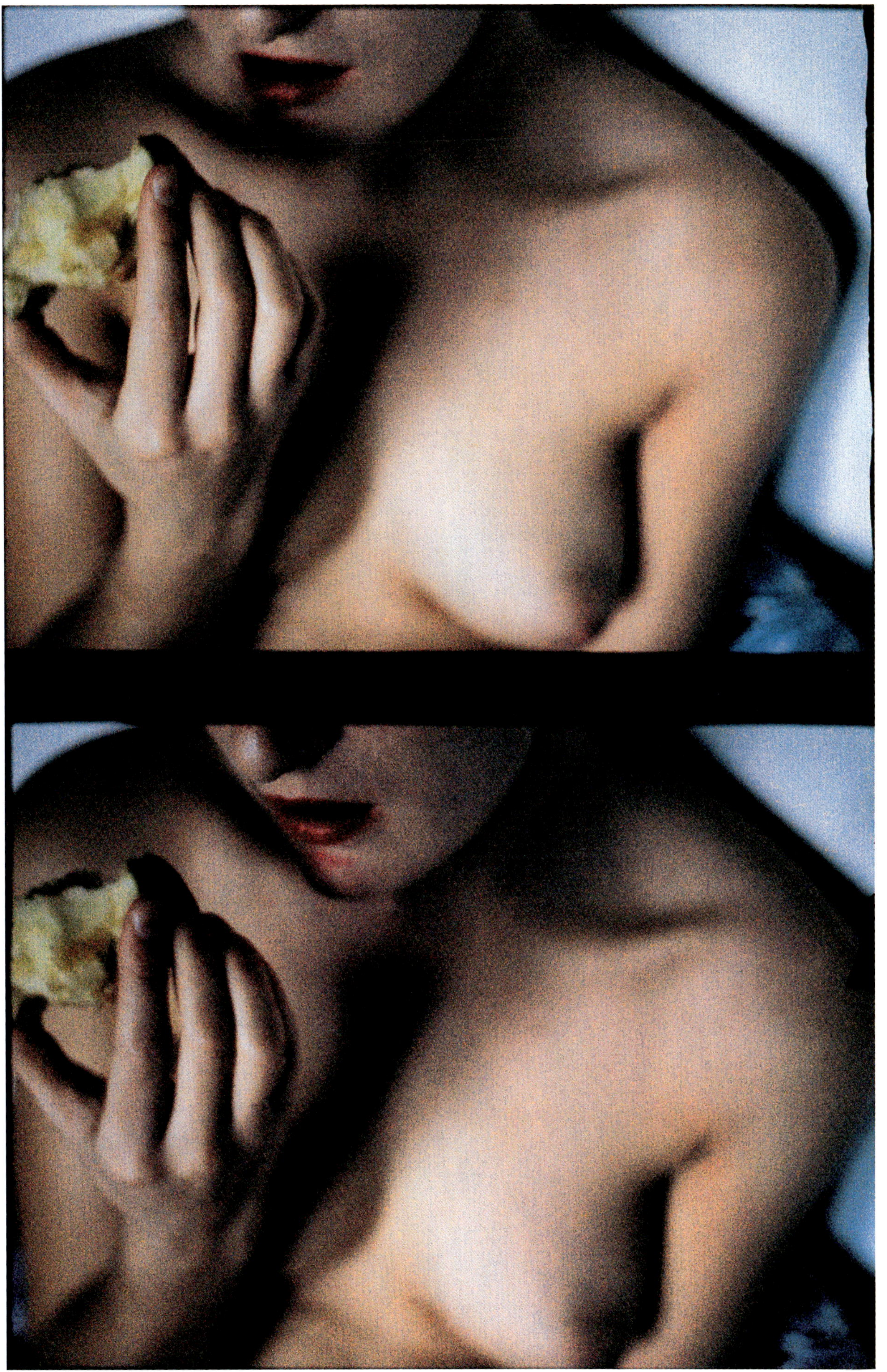

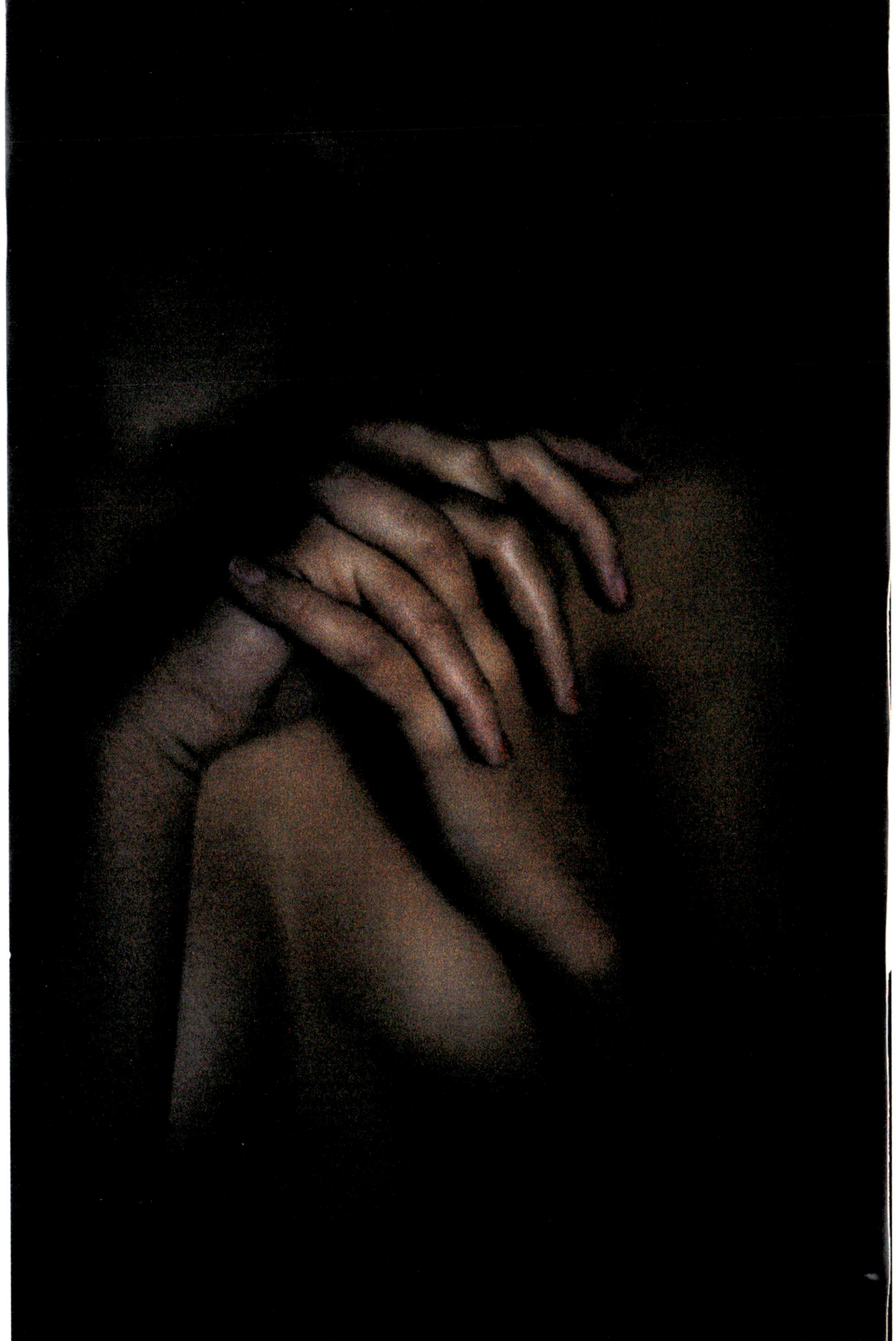

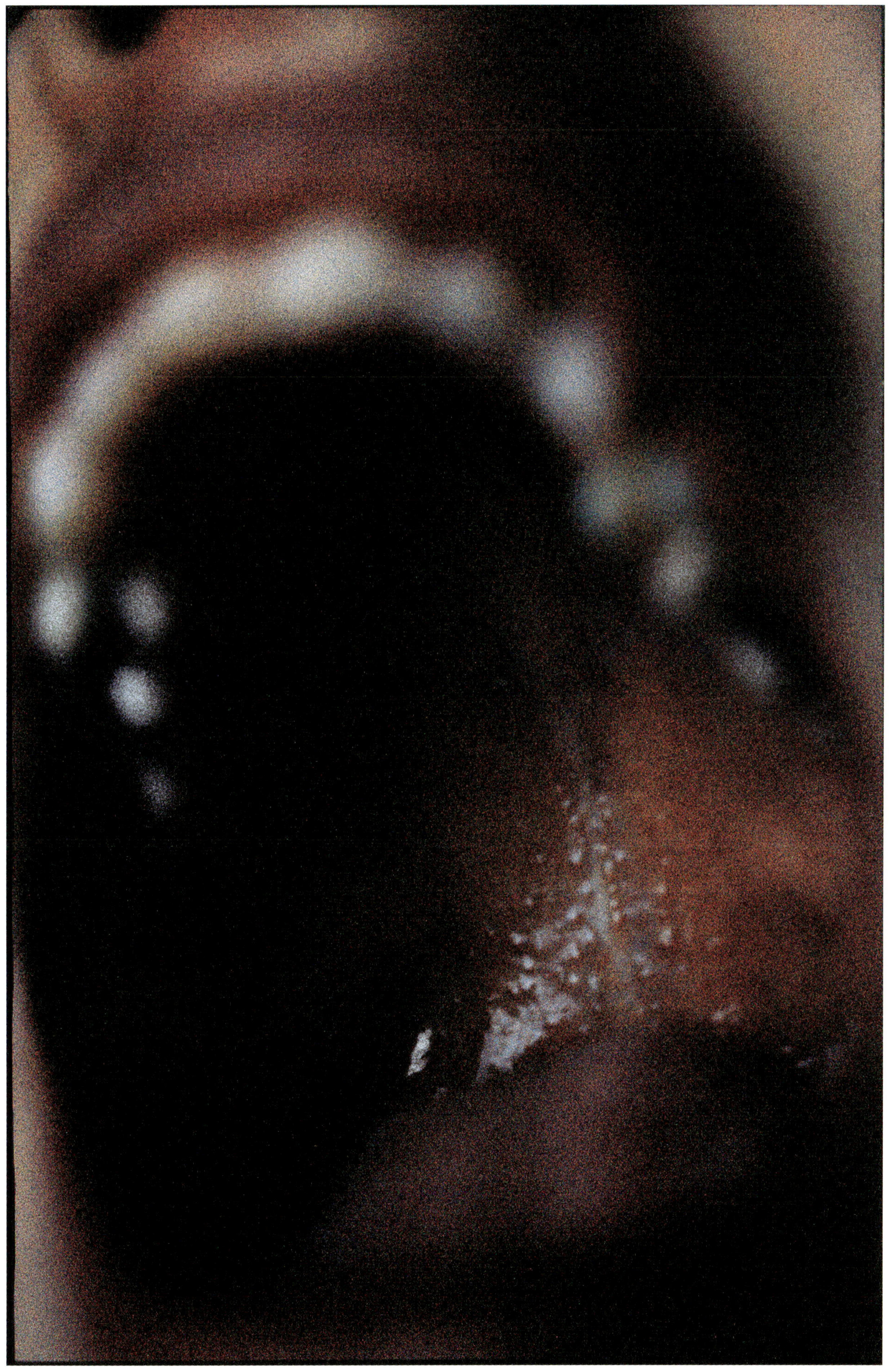

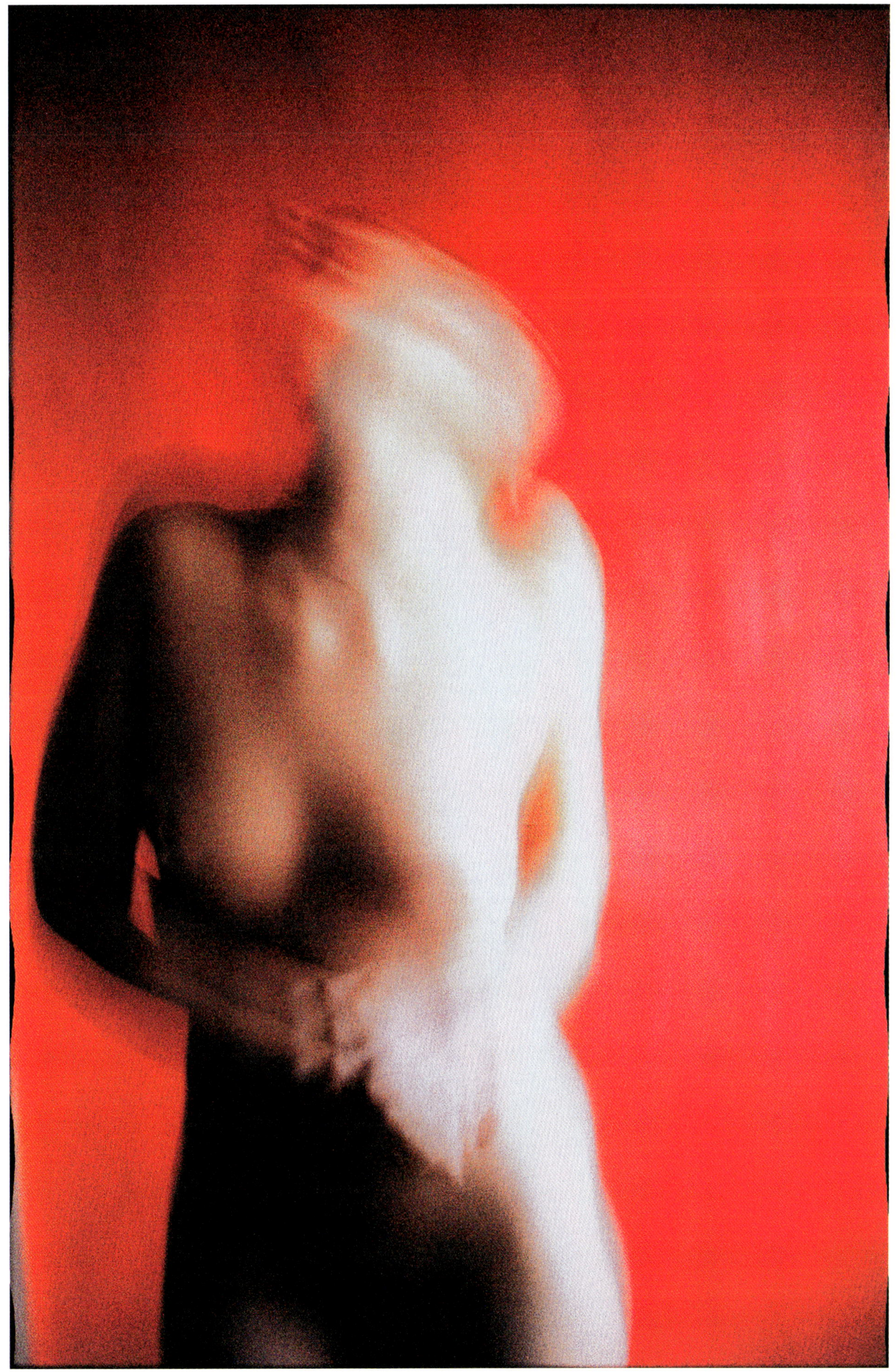

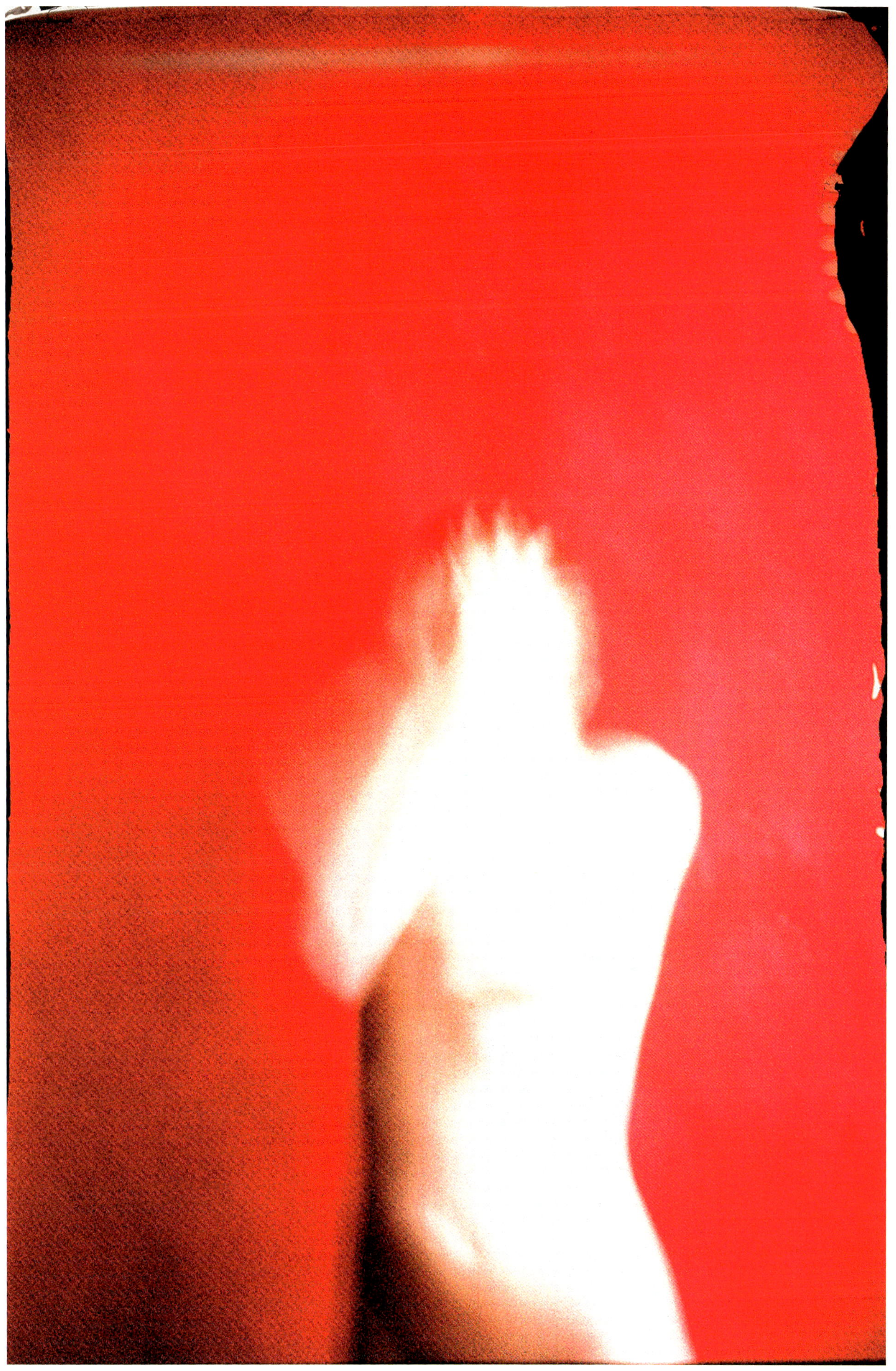

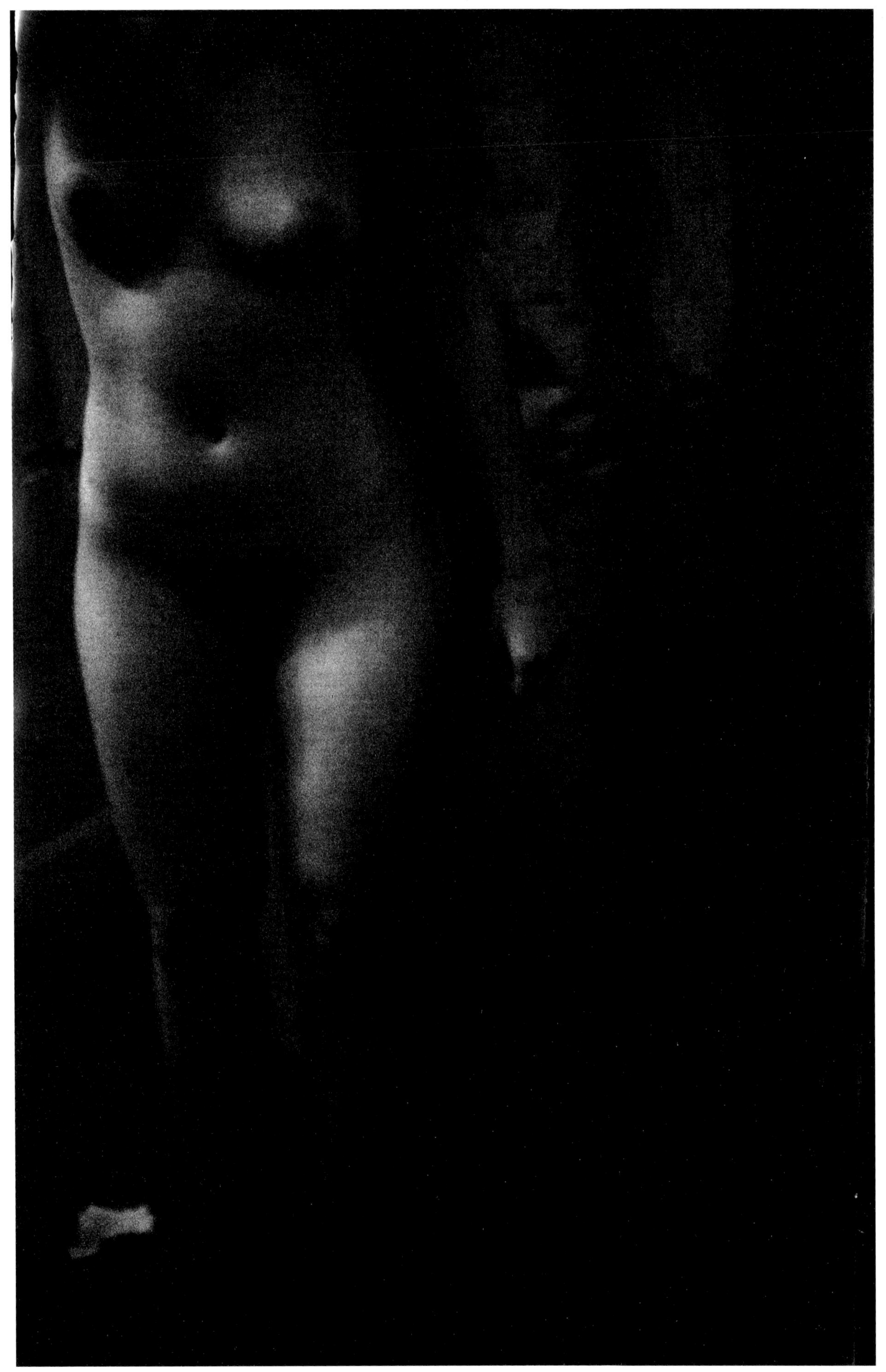

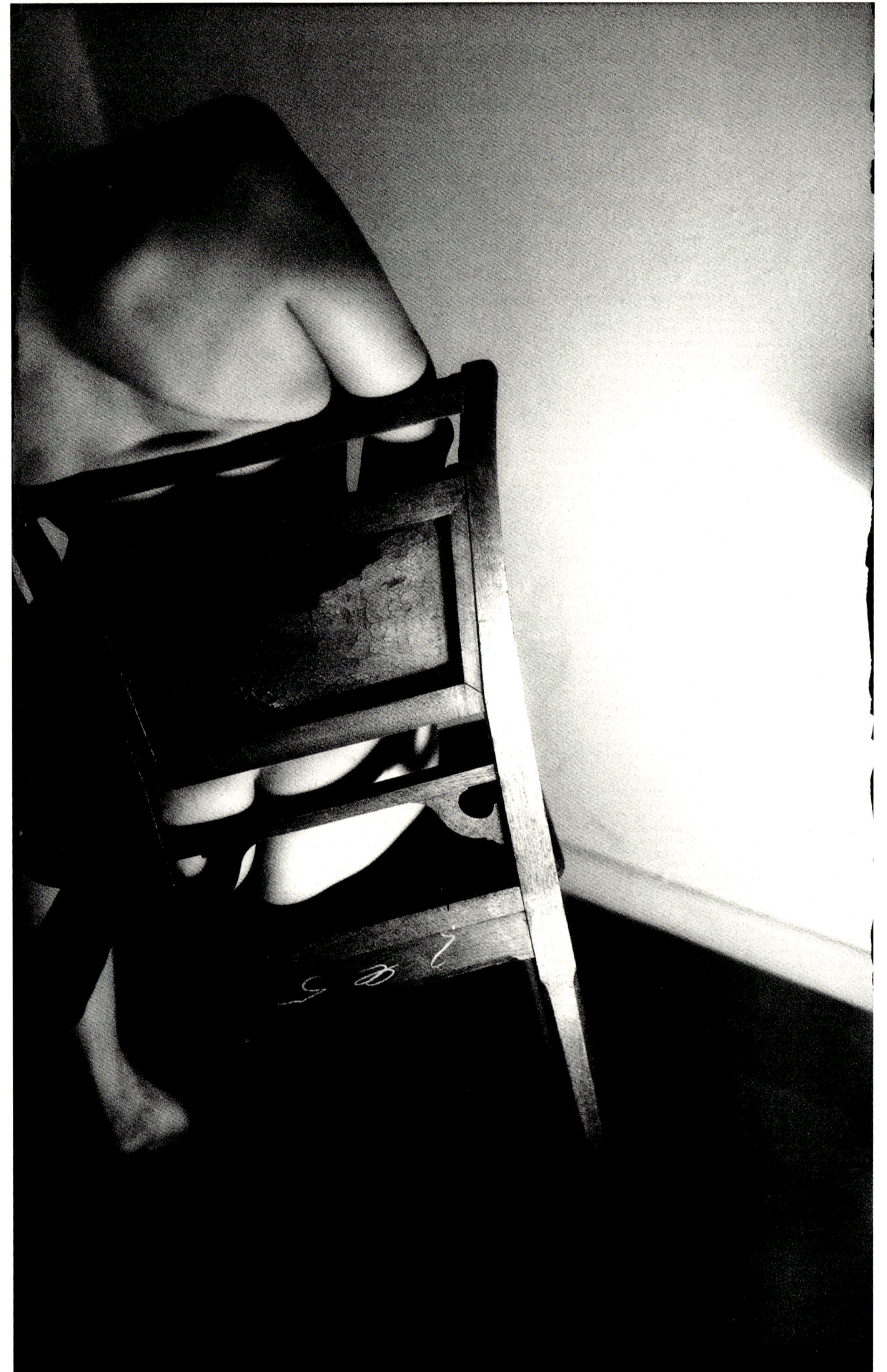

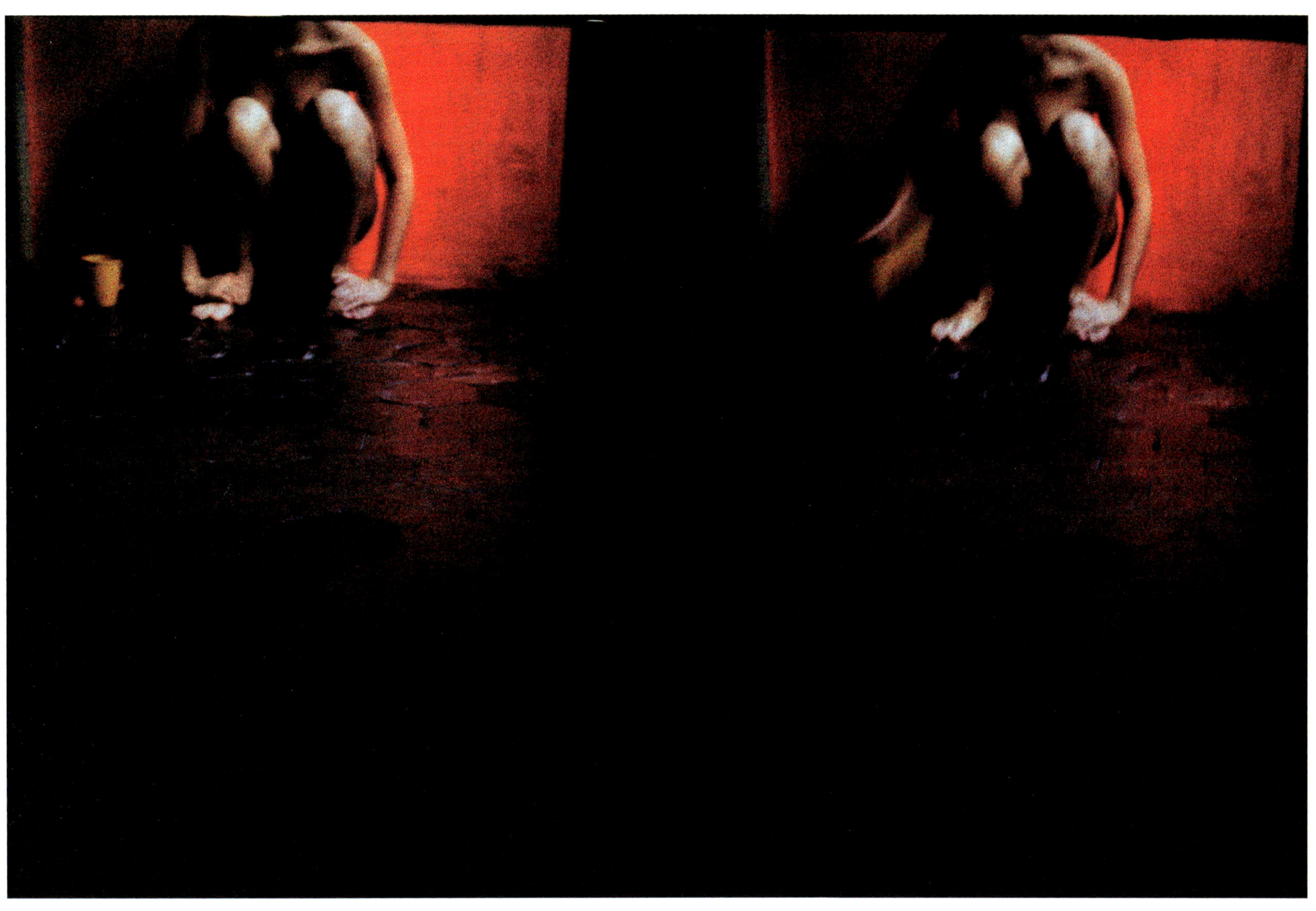

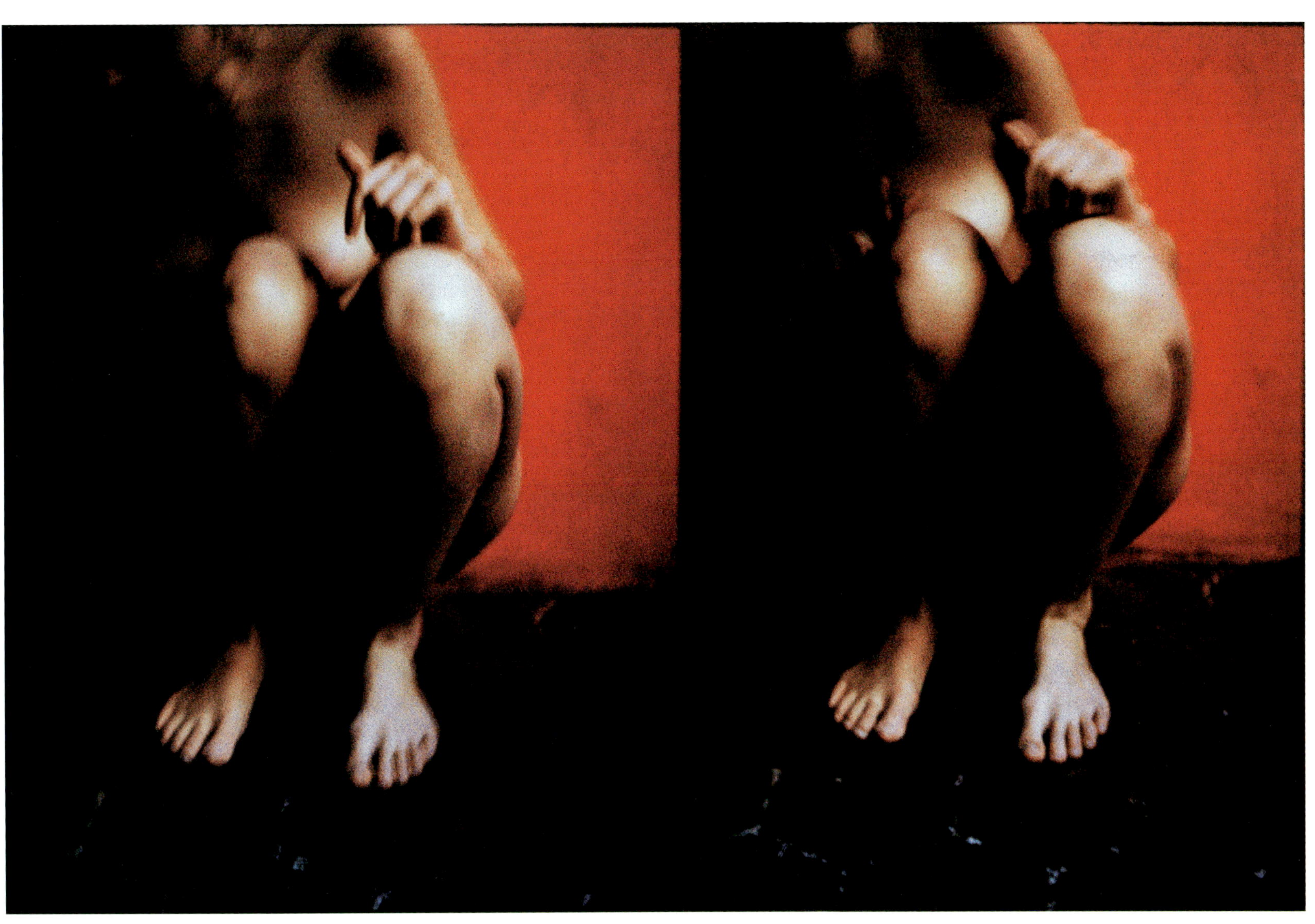

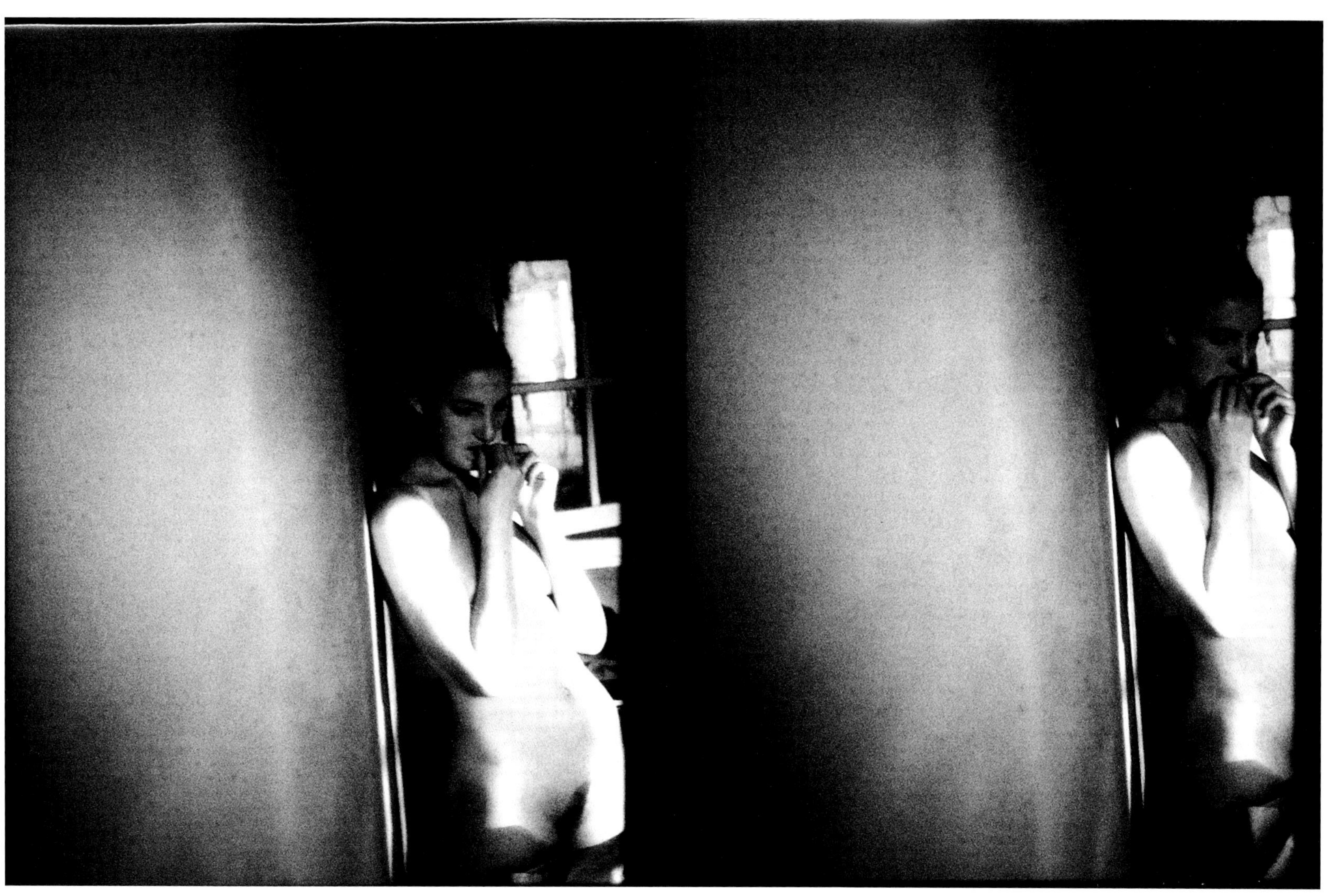

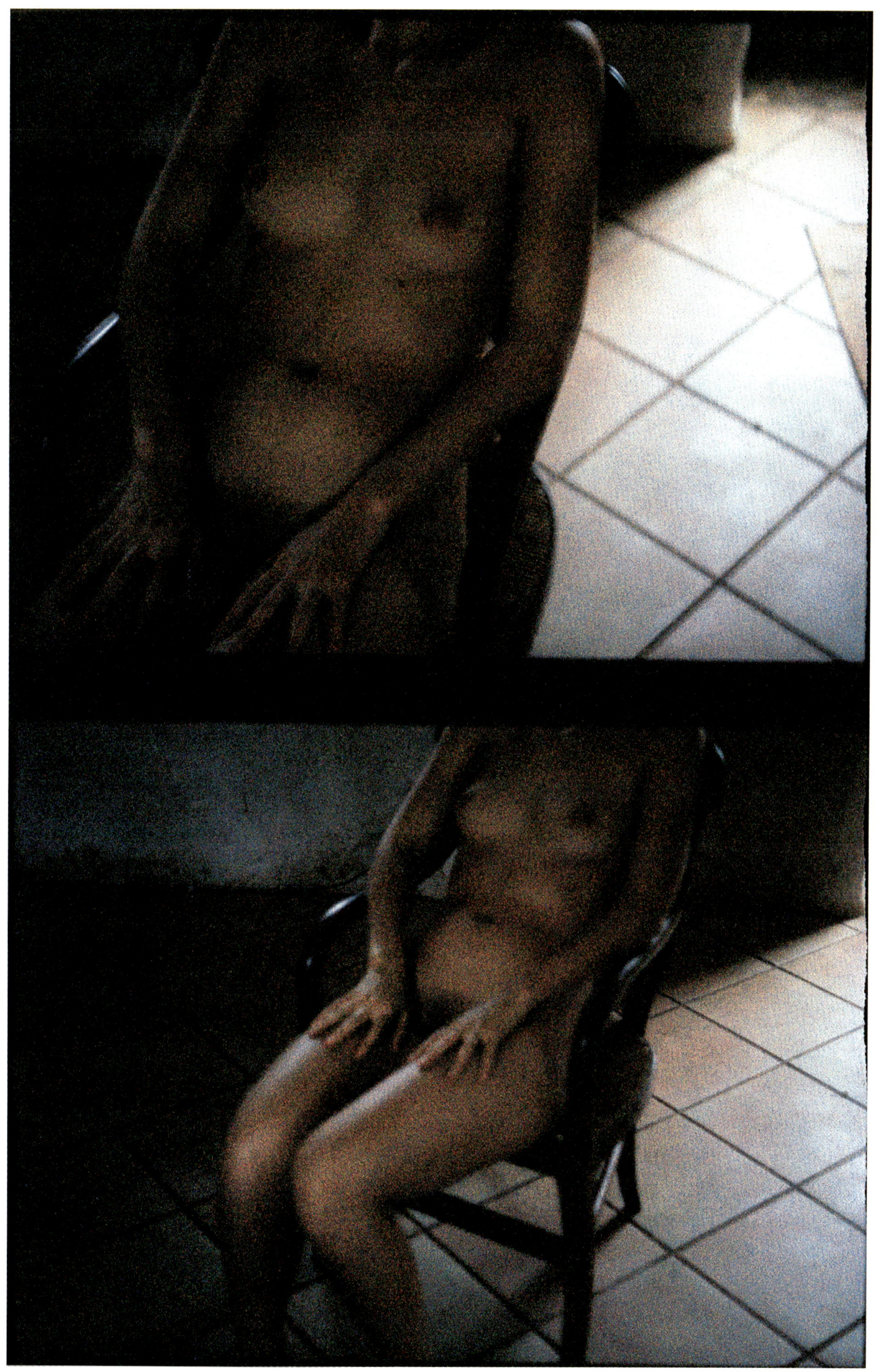

Ornela Vorpsi would especially like to thank:
Lola D'Haese, Sophie Davesne, Jacqueline Haenner, Ana J., Sabine Pera, and Cristina A.

Ornela Vorpsi – Nothing Obvious
Edited by Ornela Vorpsi and Martin Jaeggi
Bookdesign: Ornela Vorpsi, Martin Jaeggi, Gerhard Steidl
Separations, printing: Steidl, Göttingen
© 2001 for the photographs and the text: Ornela Vorpsi
© 2001 for this edition: Scalo Zurich–Berlin–New York
Head office: Weinbergstrasse 22a, CH-8001 Zurich/Switzerland,
phone +41 1 261 0910, fax +41 1 261 9262,
e-mail publishers@scalo.com, website www.scalo.com
Distributed in North America by D.A.P., New York City;
in Europe, Africa and Asia by Thames and Hudson, London;
in Germany, Austria and Switzerland by Scalo.

First Edition 2001
ISBN 3-908247-32-2
Printed in Germany